THE NATIONAL GUITAR WORKSHOP'S
JAZZ SKILLS
FILLING THE GAPS FOR THE SERIOUS GUITARIST

National Guitar
Workshop Method

Approved Curriculum

Acquisition and editorial: Nathaniel Gunod

Music typesetting: Joe Bouchard

Cover and internal design: Timothy Phelps

Chord and scale illustrations: Margo Farnsworth

Recorded and engineered by Darrel Ashley at Studio-9, CA

Cover Photo: Gary Gunderson

Book: ISBN 1-929395-10-8

Book and CD: ISBN 1-929395-11-6 .

CD: ISBN 1-929395-12-4

TABLE OF CONTENTS

ABOUT THE AUTHOR

Jody Fisher has worked professionally in virtually all styles of music during his career, from straight ahead and contemporary jazz to rock'n'roll, country and pop. He taught Guitar and Jazz Studies at the University of Redlands and Idyllwild School of Music and the Arts (ISOMATA). An active performer in the Southern California area, he still maintains a private teaching practice and is a director of the National Guitar Summer Workshop.

PHOTO–BRIAN MAURER

Other instructional products
by Jody Fisher:

Beginning Jazz Guitar (video)
Chord and Scale Finder
Jazz Guitar Christmas
Jazz Guitar Masterclass
      (with Joe Diorio, Mark Whitfield,
      Ron Escheté, Scott Henderson
      and Steve Khan)
Rhythm Guitar Encyclopedia
Stand Alone Tracks: Smooth Jazz
The Complete Jazz Guitar Method:
      Beginning Jazz Guitar
      Intermediate Jazz Guitar
      Mastering Jazz Guitar: Chord/Melody
      Mastering Jazz Guitar: Improvisation
The Guitar Mode Encyclopedia
30-Day Guitar Workout

JAZZ SKILLS

INTRODUCTION

This book is based on two one-week seminars I conduct for the National Guitar Workshop called "Jazz Skills." "Jazz Skills 1" is primarily for the rock and blues guitarist who is interested in learning some jazz basics. "Jazz Skills 2" is geared toward the jazz player looking for some more advanced concepts and techniques. Both seminars are designed to help the player gain perspective on theory and the skills required to develop an individual voice as a jazz guitarist.

Every student is unique and every class moves in its own direction, but there are always four areas of study everybody wants to learn more about. They are:

Chords and Harmony
Improvisation
Technique
Reading

During a week-long seminar, many other topics like practicing, repertoire, ear training, attitude and career paths are also discussed. In this book, we will talk about the "big four" listed above.

The ideas discussed in this book are based on the most frequently asked questions in these seminars. The "answers" are presented as an overview and are intended to inspire you to further investigation on your own. My other books delve into all of these concepts in more detail.

The "Chords and Harmony" section should give you a good perspective on jazz harmony for guitar and tie together whatever "loose ends" you may have in your understanding. Chord/melody ideas are also discussed, along with walking bass lines.

The emphasis in the "Improvisation" section is on various tools the improviser needs including scales, arpeggios, licks, melodic patterns and ways to come up with unique musical ideas over diatonic and altered chord changes.

In the "Better Technique" section, you will find various exercises that will help in all areas of guitar playing and possibly correct a few bad habits along the way. These exercises come from the "workout" period we have each day of the seminar.

While this is not really a "reading method," the "Reading" section is full of exercises and tips to help promote better skills and attitudes about this important area of guitar playing.

No single book, video or teacher will turn you into a great jazz guitarist. But working through this book should give you some perspective on the skills that are needed to become a more complete jazz guitarist.

Enjoy!

SECTION I — CHORDS & HARMONY

THE MAJOR SCALE

One of the first jazz skills to learn is how to recite the notes in all twelve major scales away from your guitar. Learn them in *circle of 4ths* order (C, F, B♭, E♭, A♭, D♭, G♭, B, E, A, D, G—each new key is a perfect 4th, five half steps, away from the last). Think about it this way:

When traveling through the circle, remember that the C scale has no sharps or flats. After that, each scale's number of flats will increase by one—F = one flat, B♭ = two flats, E♭ = three flats and so on, until you get to G♭, which has six flats (every note is flat except F). The magic number is "4." The fourth note up in each major scale tells you the name of the next scale. The fourth note up from there is the newly flatted note.

The scales B through G use sharps. Each scale decreases by one sharp—B = five sharps, E = four sharps and so on until you reach G, which has only one sharp. Once again, the magic number is "4." Now the fourth note up in every scale tells you the name of the next scale. The fourth note up from there is the newly dropped sharp.

The fourth note up in the G scale is C—that's why they call it a circle!

Below are the notes in all the major scales. Memorize them! You *really* need to do this!

Key	Notes						
C	C	D	E	F	G	A	B	C
F	F	G	A	B♭	C	D	E	F
B♭	B♭	C	D	E♭	F	G	A	B♭
E♭	E♭	F	G	A♭	B♭	C	D	E♭
A♭	A♭	B♭	C	D♭	E♭	F	G	A♭
D♭	D♭	E♭	F	G♭	A♭	B♭	C	D♭
G♭	G♭	A♭	B♭	C♭	D♭	E♭	F	G♭
B	B	C♯	D♯	E	F♯	G♯	A♯	B
E	E	F♯	G♯	A	B	C♯	D♯	E
A	A	B	C♯	D	E	F♯	G♯	A
D	D	E	F♯	G	A	B	C♯	D
G	G	A	B	C	D	E	F♯	G

Remember—no peeking at your guitar!

Here are the scales on the staff:

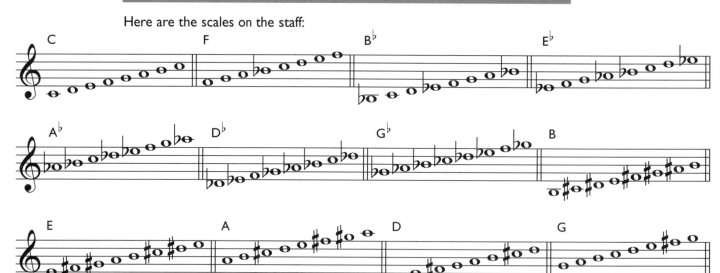

This is an area in which most players have some experience, but few have done an extensive study. The material we will cover here will help you become a better improviser, as well as give you a way to learn and catalog new chords. But first, you have a little more memorizing to do. This will be the last thing you will be asked to memorize this way. This may sound a little strange, but you need to be able to recite all twelve major triads (in circle of 4ths order) *in twelve seconds!* Yes. Time yourself. You need to be able to think fast if you are someday going to use this information while improvising.

Major triads are composed of the root, 3rd and 5th tones in any major scale (C - E - G = C Major, F - A - C = F Major, etc.).

Here they are. On your mark….get set…..

Root	3rd	5th
C	E	G
F	A	C
B♭	D	F
E♭	G	B♭
A♭	C	E♭
D♭	F	A♭
G♭	B♭	D♭
B	D♯	F♯
E	G♯	B
A	C♯	E
D	F♯	A
G	B	D

Here they are on the staff:

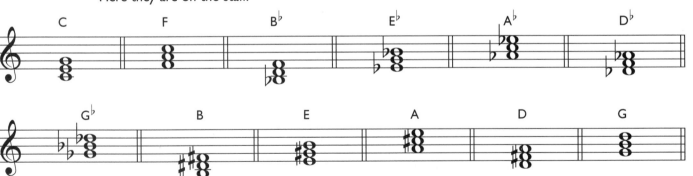

Now may be a good time to review triads just in case there are any gaps in your knowledge. Besides the major triad, there are three others: the minor, the diminished and the augmented. The chord formulas continue to reference the major scale. In other words, if the formula calls for a note altered from its normal position in the major scale, a sharp or flat will be used to indicate the difference. For example, if the formula requires a lowered 3rd, it will be shown as $^\flat$3.

The formula for the minor triad is root, $^\flat$3 and 5.

C - E$^\flat$ - G = Cmin, F - A$^\flat$ - C = Fmin, etc.

---

min = Minor
dim = Diminished
Aug = Augmented

The formula for the diminished triad is root, $^\flat$3 and $^\flat$5.

C - E$^\flat$ - G$^\flat$ = Cdim, F - A$^\flat$ - C$^\flat$ = Fdim, etc.

The formula for the augmented triad is root, 3 and $^\sharp$5.

C – E – G$^\sharp$ = CAug, F – A – C$^\sharp$ = FAug, etc.

INVERTING TRIADS

We can invert these triads. In other words, we can play the notes in each triad in any order we want and it will still be the same chord. The inversion of the triad is determined by which note is in the bass (in the lowest position).

Note in the Bass	Inversion
R	Root Position
3	1st Inversion
5	2nd Inversion

It is very important to know where all of these triads lie on the fingerboard. The following chart shows moveable forms for all the major, minor, diminished and augmented triads, in all three inversions, on four different sets of strings, all with a C root. It is very easy to transpose these to any key. Simply find the desired root on the appropriate string and move the form there. Notice that the string sets included here are all adjacent strings: 6-5-4, 5-4-3, 4-3-2 and 3-2-1. Fret numbers are shown on the left, and suggested fingerings are shown across the top. An × indicates not to play that string. Try these in all keys.

TRIADS ON FOUR STRING SETS

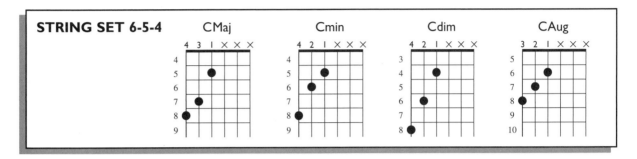

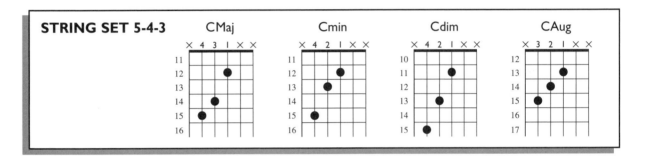

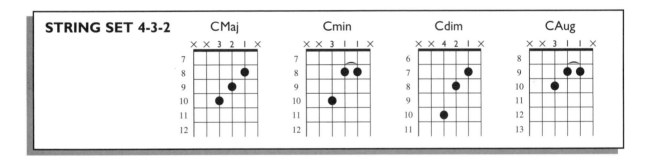

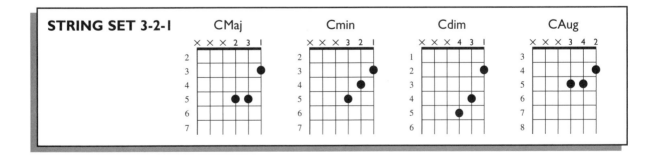

There are many ways to develop a huge chord vocabulary and this book will cover several. As long as we are talking about triads, here is a way to learn new chords based on the triad shapes you have just learned.

Let's say we wanted to build major 6 chords. The formula for a major 6 chord is R-3-5-6. We have twelve different major triad shapes (three inversions x four string sets = twelve). Let's put this information together and see what we come up with.

We'll build a C6 chord so the notes will be C-E-G-A (this is one reason you want to memorize your scales and triads!). Play a root position C triad on the highest string set (3-2-1). We already have the C, the E and the G, so now look around for an A to add to it. Well, what do you know! There's an A on the 4th string at the 7th fret. Add it to the triad and you have a nice C6 chord.

The following example shows that many C6 chords based on triad shapes are just waiting to be found. The string set for each C Major triad is indicated.

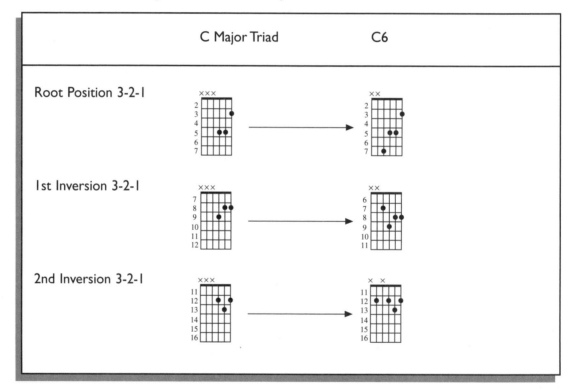

JAZZ
SKILLS

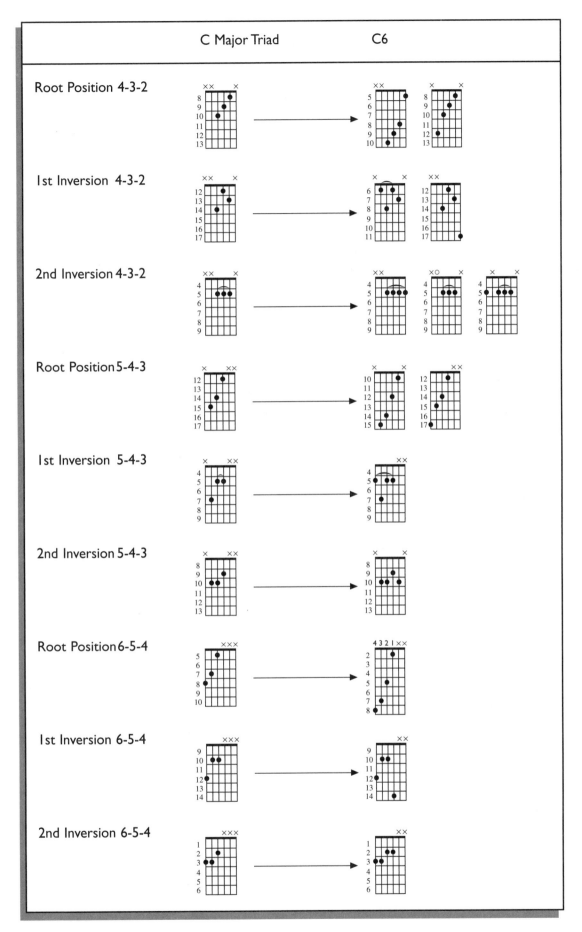

In case you didn't know this, a C6 chord has exactly the same notes in it as an A Minor 7 (Amin7). This is what is known as a *chord synonym*. Most chords are synonyms of others.

Be sure to try this with many different types.

HARMONIZED SCALES

Harmonizing a scale is another good way to generate more chords. When we harmonize a scale, we generally stack 3rds on top of each scale degree, using only notes found in the scale. For that reason, we can think of these as the *diatonic* harmonies of the scale. Diatonic means "belonging to the scale or key." We will stack three tones above each scale degree in the following examples to produce 7 chords. A 7 chord is a four-note chord that includes a triad plus a note a 7th above the root. When we harmonize with four-note chords, we get some interesting chords. The formulas will be provided as we go. Be sure to transpose the following harmonizations to all twelve keys.

In the following written examples, all chords are in root position. For practical reasons, the fingerings shown above the music are not in root position. Generally, we generate these chord scales by starting with the first chord and then moving each voice in the chord up to the next scale tone on the same string.

HARMONIZING A G MAJOR SCALE

Results in major 7 (Maj7: 1-3-5-7), minor 7 (min7: 1-♭3-5-♭7), dominant 7 (7: 1-3-5-♭7) and minor 7♭5 (min7♭5: 1-♭3-♭5-♭7).

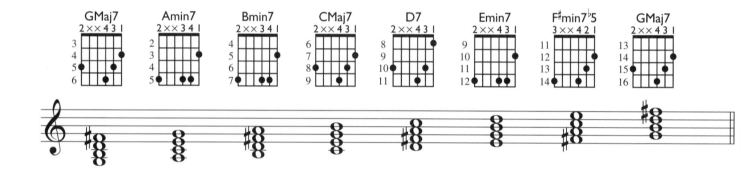

HARMONIZING A C MELODIC MINOR SCALE

Results in minor/major 7 (min/Maj7: 1-♭3-5-7), minor 7, major 7♯5 (Maj7♯5: 1-3-♯5-7), dominant 7 and minor 7♭5.

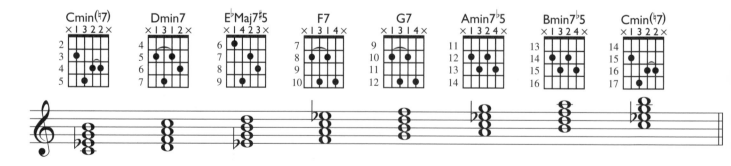

JAZZ
SKILLS

HARMONIZING A C HARMONIC MINOR

Results in minor/major 7, minor 7♭5, major 7♯5, minor 7, dominant 7, major 7 and diminished 7 (1-♭3-♭5-♭♭7*).

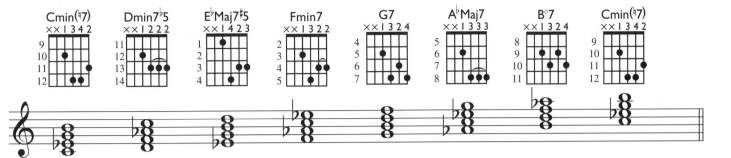

*♭♭ = *Double flat.* Lower the note one whole step.

MOVING CHORDS ACROSS STRING SETS

Another way to learn new chords is to move chords across the string sets. There are two ways to think about this.

A. Start with a chord voicing that lies on a high set of strings and find the exact same voicing on other string sets. In other words, if your original *voicing* (arrangement of pitches) lies on strings 1-2-3-4, try to find it on strings 2-3-4-5 and then 3-4-5-6. Here is an example taking the same voicings of GMaj7 and C7 across several sets of strings.

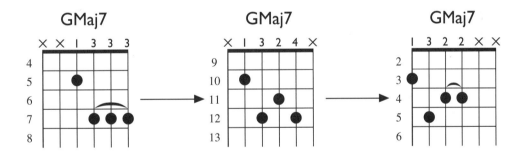

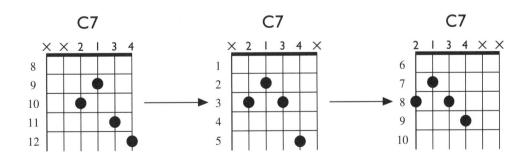

B. Start with a chord shape on a particular set of strings. Then maintain the *shape* (form) of the chord and move it over to the next string set. If it's possible to move it again, do so. Obviously, the chord type will change but this may introduce you to some interesting new voicings using a shape you are already used to. Look what happens to CMaj7 and Gmin7 when you move them across the string sets.

CMaj7

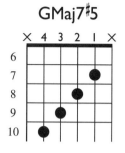

GMaj7♯5

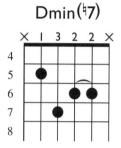

DAug

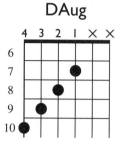

Gmin7

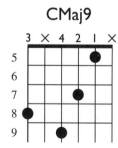

Dmin(♮7)

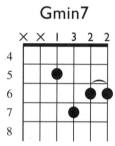

AMaj7

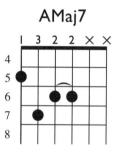

MOVING VOICES

This is simply a matter of starting with a particular chord voicing and experimenting by moving some of the tones around to see what you come up with.

Here is a CMaj9 chord (1-3-7-9):

CMaj9

By moving some of the voices of this CMaj9 chord around, you could come up with some other interesting sounds. The diagram shows changes that result in the following chords:

Chord	Formula
C Major 13	1-3-7-9-13 (a 13 is just an octave above the 6)
C7♭9	1-3-♭7-♭9
C11	1-♭7-9-11 (an 11 is just an octave above the 4)
C13sus	1-♭7-9-11-13

CMaj13
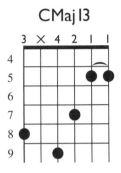

C9
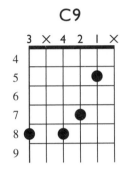

C7♭9
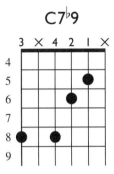

C11
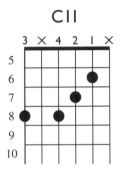

C13sus
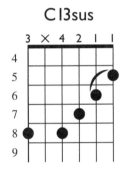

Cmin9
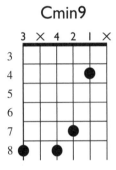

Another related idea would be to switch any note on the low E string to the high E string, and vice versa.

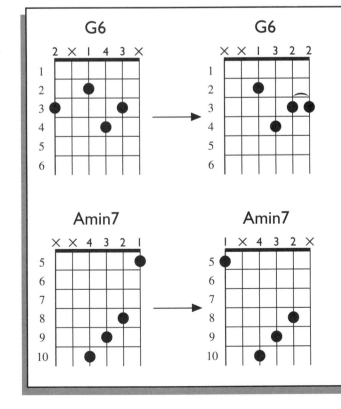

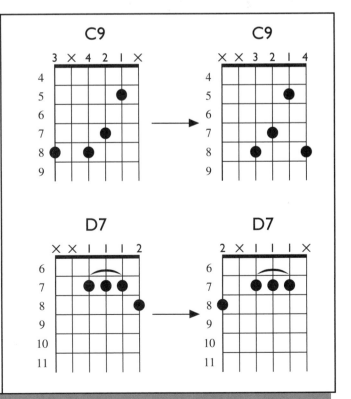

ALTERED CHORDS

If you are interested in this material, you should already have a basic understanding of diatonic chord formulas. If you don't, take a look at *Beginning Jazz Guitar* (Alfred #14120) to brush up on this information—it's easy and won't take too long. The following won't make much sense to you without this background. It might also help to review the scale harmonizations on page 12 of this book.

Altered chords are usually a source of confusion for beginning jazz players, and even more experienced guitar players sometimes lack a good overview of the subject. Before we get to some actual altered chord voicings, let's start with some background information.

A chord is said to be altered when one or more of its tones has been raised or lowered a half step. This adds non-diatonic notes to the original chord. Major, minor and dominant chords can all be altered, but we tend to alter dominant chords the most.

Only 5ths and 9ths can really be altered. If you try to alter any other note in the scale, it either becomes an altered 5 or 9, or becomes a redundancy within the chord. Watch what happens:

Possible Alterations		
Raising the root	=	♭9
Lowering the 2nd	=	♭9
Raising the 2nd	=	♯9
Lowering the 3rd	=	♯9
Raising the 3rd	=	4th or 11th (same thing, not an altered tone)
Lowering the 4th	=	3rd (not an altered tone)
Raising the 4th	=	♭5
Lowering the 5th	=	♭5 (obviously)
Raising the 5th	=	♯5 (obviously)
Lowering the 6th	=	♯5
Raising the 6th	=	♭7 (essential tone for dominant chords, not an altered tone)
Lowering the 7th	=	♭7
Raising the 7th	=	root

So you see, the only real alterations possible are ♭5, ♯5, ♭9 and ♯9. There are chords with a ♯11. But the ♯11 is the same as the ♭5 an octave higher. Because of range limitations of the instrument, guitarists sometimes think of the ♭5 and ♯11 as interchangeable.

So when you think about it at its most basic level, altered dominant chords have these eight possibilities:

7♭5	7♭5♭9
7♯5	7♯5♯9
7♭9	7♭5♯9
7♯9	7♯5♭9

- A natural 9, 11 and 13 can be added to any chord with an altered 5.
- 11ths and 13ths can be added to chords with an altered 9.
- The most common altered major chords are :
  Maj7#11 (1-3-5-7-9-#11)
  Maj7#5 (1-3-#5-7)
  Maj7♭5 (1-3-♭5-7)
- The most common altered minor chords are:
  min7♭5 (1-♭3-♭5-♭7) This is actually a diatonic chord, too.
  min7#5 (1-♭3-#5-♭7)

That's pretty much the story. Remember that coming up with cool and unusual voicings is where most of the fun is when working with altered chords. The rest of this section will show examples of these chords and include some other ideas about them.

ALTERED CHORD CONCEPTS

7♭5 CHORDS (1-3-♭5-♭7)

One interesting thing about 7♭5 chords is that, through the marvels of enharmonic respellings, each voicing is actually two different 7♭5 chords whose roots are a ♭5 apart. For example, C7♭5 and G♭7♭5 can be played with the same voicing because, if you respell two of them, all the notes are identical.

C7♭5 (C-E-G♭-B♭) = G♭7♭5 (G♭-B♭-D♭♭-F♭)

D♭♭ = C and F♭ = E

The two chords are spelled differently but they sound the same.

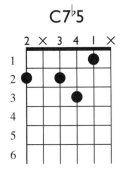
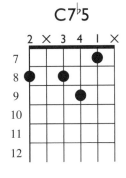
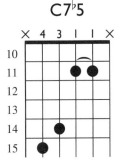
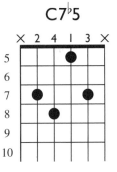

7#5 CHORDS (1-3-5#-♭7)

This chord has a very distinctive sound, and it is easy to find new voicings for it. The augmented triad, which is the basis for a 7#5, repeats itself every major 3rd up the fingerboard. Again, through the wizardry of enharmonic respellings, a C#aug, Eaug and G#aug are all the same. Simply add a ♭7 to an augmented triad and you have a 7#5 chord.

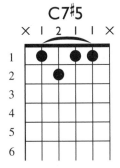
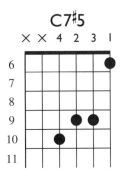

7♭9 CHORDS (1-5-♭7-♭9)

A 7♭9 chord voiced without a root (3-5-♭7-♭9) is the same as a diminished 7 chord (1-♭3-♭5-♭♭7) whose root is a major 3rd higher. Since diminished 7 chords repeat themselves every minor 3rd in much the same way that augmented triads repeat themselves every major 3rd (once again, thanks to enharmonic respellings), we can say the same for rootless 7♭9 voicings. Just practice moving your rootless 7♭9 chords around in minor 3rds and watch your vocabulary for this altered chord expand.

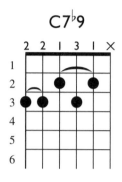
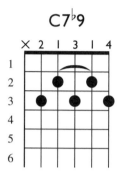
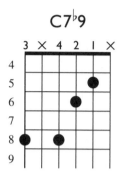
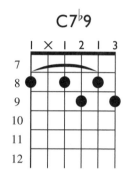

7♯9 CHORDS (1-5-♭7-♯9)

We all know and love this chord. It is not true that Jimi Hendrix invented it.

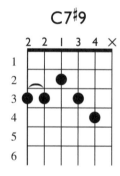
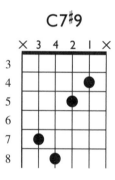
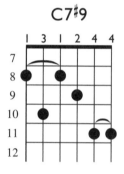
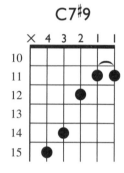

7♭5♭9 CHORDS (1-♭5-♭7-♭9)

A 7♭5♭9 chord voiced without a root (♭5-♭7-♭9-3) is the same as a dominant 7 chord (1-3-5-♭7) whose root is a ♭5 above. For example, a rootless C7♭5♭9 voicing is also G♭7.

Rootless C7♭5♭9 (G♭-B♭-D♭-E) = G♭7 (G♭-B♭-D♭-F♭)

F♭ = E

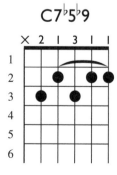
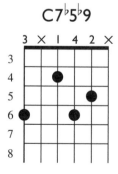
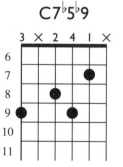
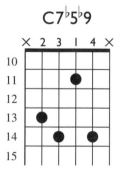

At first, all these rules may seem a little overwhelming. But if you study them one at a time, they become little blessings instead of curses!

7#5#9 CHORDS (1-#5-♭7-#9)

When using chords with multiple alterations, such as 7♭5♭9 and 7#5#9, be careful that the altered tones do not conflict with the melody of the tune!

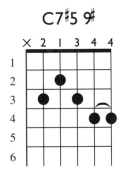

C7#5 9#

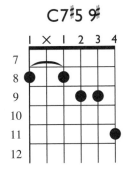

C7#5 9#

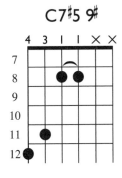

C7#5 9#

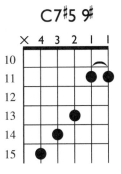

C7#5 9#

7♭5#9 (1-♭5-♭7-#9)

This chord has a nice, spicy sound.

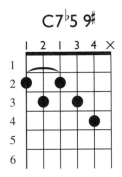

C7♭5 9#

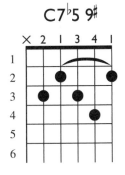

C7♭5 9#

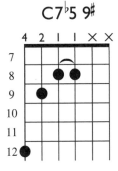

C7♭5 9#

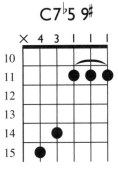

C7♭5 9#

7#5♭9 CHORDS (1-#5-♭7-♭9)

A rootless 7#5♭9 voicing is the same as a min7♭5 chord a whole step below. For example, a rootless C7#5♭9 is the same as B♭min7♭5.

Rootless C7#5♭9 (E-G#-B♭-D♭) = B♭min7♭5 (B♭-D♭-F♭-A♭)

F♭ = E and A♭ = G#

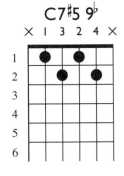

C7#5 9♭

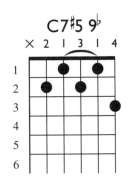

C7#5 9♭

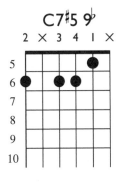

C7#5 9♭

C7#5 9♭

This is an interesting idea that will significantly widen your musical choices. It should be explored with all types of chords. In *symmetrical chord movement*, a specific chord shape on the fingerboard is moved at a set interval up the fingerboard. We continue to think of the same root, the *function* remains the same (for example, dominant remains dominant), but the frets, extensions and alterations change.

Let's start with $7^\flat5$ chords. Dominant $7^\flat5$ chords retain their dominant function when they are moved around the fingerboard in intervals of whole steps.

Here is a $C7^\flat5$:

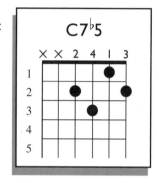

If you base your thinking on the original chord's root, you will produce the following chords as you move the form up by whole steps:

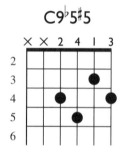 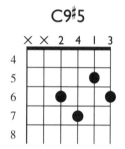 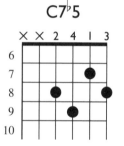 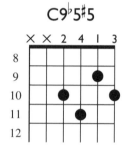 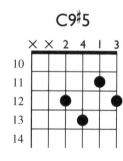

It is interesting that all the chords produced have an altered 5th. Some of them have 9ths as well. You get the same chords if you start with a dominant 9th or a $7^\sharp5$:

STARTING WITH C9

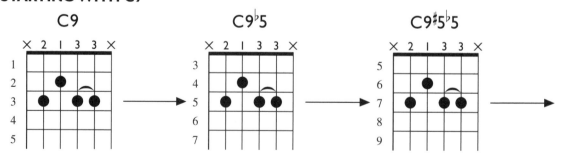

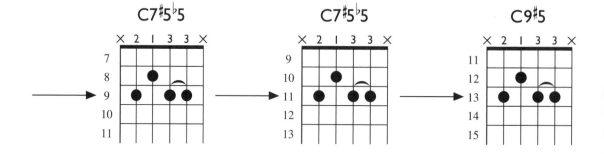

JAZZ
SKILLS

STARTING WITH C7♯5

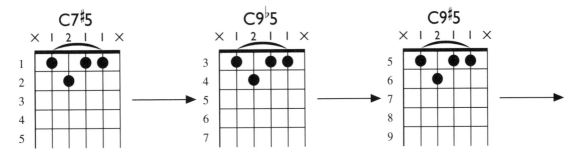

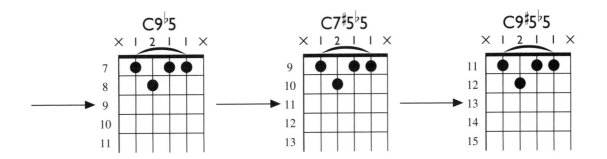

Another interesting thing is that you can consider *any* of the notes in the chord to be the root.

Here's how that works out:

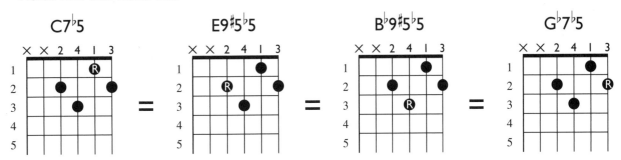

You *still* get dominant chords with altered 5ths, with or without a 9th.

If you can consider any of the notes in the chord to be the root, you can still move them around in whole steps. The same thing happens: you get even more dominant chords with altered 5ths.

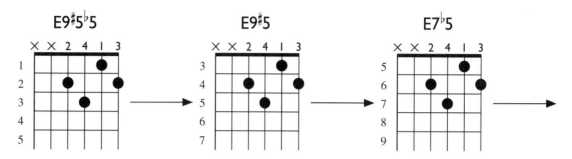

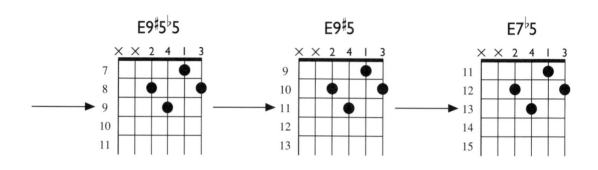

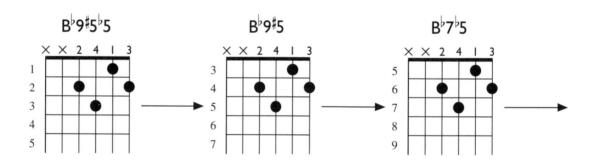

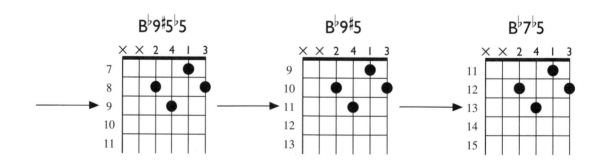

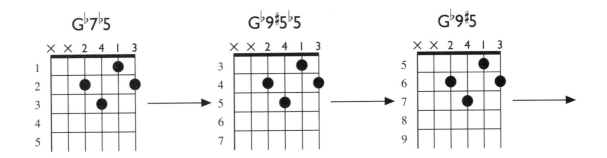

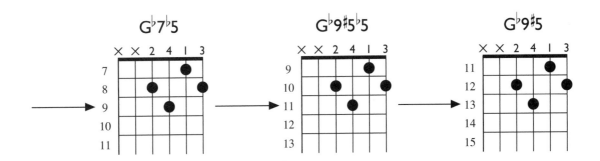

How to Use This Concept

Whenever you need an altered chord, you simply need to grab one of these shapes making sure that the appropriate root is contained in the chord! Of course, some chords could sound much better than others in a given context. Experimentation is necessary.

Here are a few ii-V7-I progressions to demonstrate this idea:

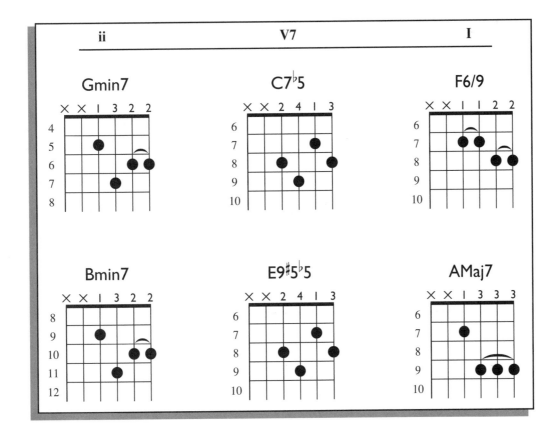

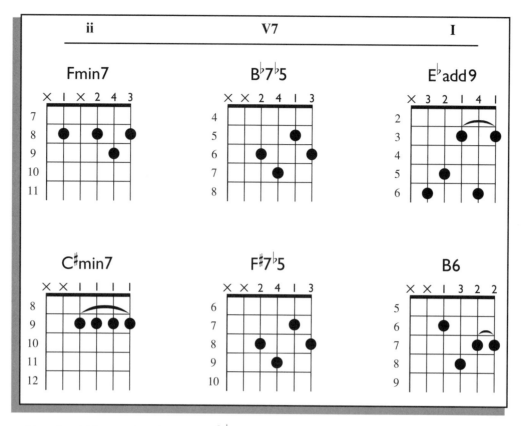

You should know that dominant 7♯5♭5 chords are also commonly referred to as dominant 7♭5♭13 chords—the ♯5 is enharmonically respelled as ♭13.

CHORD MELODY BASICS

Chord/melody describes a style of guitar playing where a song's melody is played with a combination of chords and single notes. Generally, the melody will be the highest note in a chord. Some players like to harmonize much of the melody and others prefer an approach that is a little lighter—chords are used more sparingly. By the same token, some players enjoy large and harmonically rich harmonies while others like to imply harmonies with smaller chords. It comes down to experience and taste.

This section will touch upon some of the important key areas. *Mastering Jazz Guitar: Chord/Melody* from *The Complete Jazz Guitar Method* really digs deep into this subject and will help you with the more complex areas of chord/melody arranging. Once you have the basics, being a good chord/melody arranger is really a matter of knowing many different arranging techniques. Many of the techniques that are used in band and orchestral arrangements work equally well on the guitar.

The most basic skill to master is recognizing chord tones in the melody. In the beginning, you should try to harmonize the chord tones in any given melody with chords you already know. It will soon become apparent that you probably need to learn more interesting chords. Learning new chords for a chord/melody arrangement is one of the best ways to accumulate new voicings quickly. By practicing the song, you are also practicing the new voicings. I've always tried to incorporate new voicings in every new tune I learn. After you've learned many songs, you start to accumulate many voicings as well.

Here is a melody with some chord changes shown above the staff:

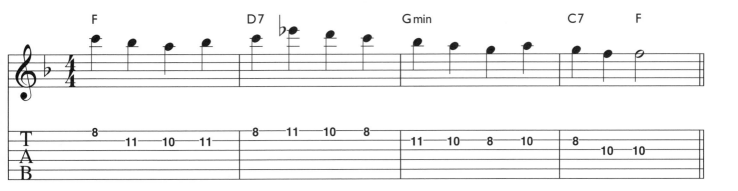

Here are two possible ways to harmonize this melody using these chords:

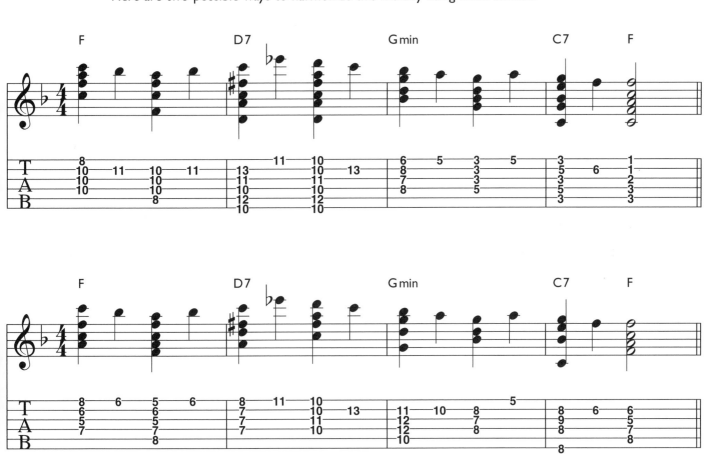

CHORD ENHANCEMENT

When you are ready to go beyond the basic chords given to you in books and sheet music, the next step is thinking about *chord enhancement*. Most chords can be thought of as being a member of one of three basic chord families: major, minor or dominant. You enhance a chord when you add extensions (9, 11, 13) or replace it with another chord from the same family. The root doesn't change—just the flavor of the chord. In other words, playing a C6, CMaj7, CMaj9, CMaj13 or any other C Major-type chord could enhance a simple C triad. The same idea carries over to minor and dominant chords as well.

The following list should give you a good start enhancing your basic chords. Remember that context is *everything*. Just because it may be theoretically correct doesn't mean that it sounds great. Like everything else, you need to experiment and gain experience.

Here are the chords of the three major chord families:

Major Chords	Minor Chords	Dominant Chords
Major Triad	minor triad	Dom7
Maj6	min6	Dom9
Maj7	min7	Dom11
Maj9	min9	Dom13
Maj13	min11	Dom7/6
Maj add9	min13	Dom7/11
Maj7/6	min add9	Dom7sus
Maj6/9	min7/11	Dom9sus
	min6/9	Dom7$\flat$5
		Dom7$\sharp$5
		Dom7$\flat$9
		Dom7$\sharp$9
		Dom7$\sharp$5$\sharp$9
		Dom7$\flat$5$\flat$9
		Dom7$\flat$5$\sharp$9
		Dom7$\sharp$5$\flat$9
		Dom13$\flat$9

JAZZ SKILLS

Here are two more harmonizations for the melody introduced on page 25 using chord enhancement:

Chord enhancement is not the same thing as chord substitution. Chord substitution is replacing one chord with another chord that has a different root. When you enhance a chord, the root remains the same.

GUIDELINES FOR ARRANGING

1. Generally, you will have to raise the melody an octave if you are learning the song from a book or sheet music.
2. Try arranging the song in a key other than the one it was written in. It's often possible to create beautiful effects using open string voicings that another key may suggest.
3. Memorize the melody in single notes first. Be able to play it all over the fingerboard and in different registers.
4. Memorize the chord changes and be able to play them all over the fingerboard.
5. Arrange your song with basic chords first. After you can do that proficiently, try to dress up the arrangement with chord enhancements and other arranging techniques we will discuss, such as substitutions and passing chords.
6. Keep your arrangements loose. Eventually you'll want to improvise in this style. Constantly update and apply new skills to your repertoire.

CHORD SUBSTITUTION

This section covers two types of chord substitution, diatonic and tritone. A strong understanding of these devices will make the study of more advanced methods much easier. There are many devices and ways to substitute chords. Many more can be found in *Mastering Jazz Guitar: Chord/Melody*.

DIATONIC SUBSTITUTION:

Diatonic substitution occurs when a chord is substituted with another chord from the same harmonized scale. For example, some of the most common substitutions for 7 chords in the key of F would be:

WRITTEN CHORD		POSSIBLE SUBSTITUTION
FMaj7	I	Dmin7, Amin7
Gmin7	ii	B♭Maj7
Amin7	iii	Dmin7
B♭Maj7	IV	Gmin7
C7	V	Emin7♭5
Dmin7	vi	FMaj7
Emin7♭5	vii	Gmin7

The reason this works is because every other 7 chord in the diatonic scale share three notes in common. Often, chords that have three or more notes in common can substitute for each other. The chart below demonstrates how every chord (oval) shares three tones with a chord one 3rd above in the key (rectangle)—in this case, F Major:

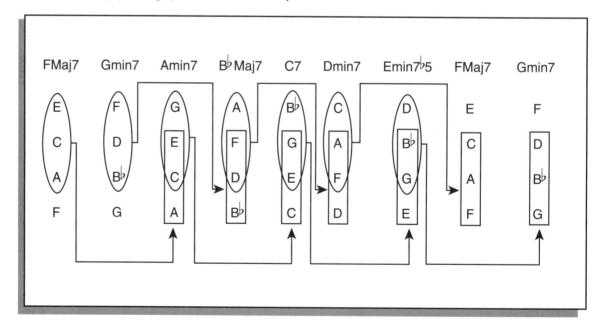

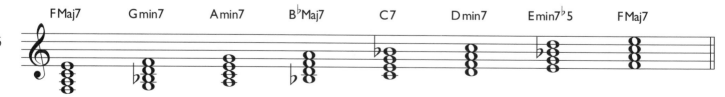

TRITONE SUBSTITUTION

When a progression travels from V7 to I, it is common to replace the V7 chord with a dominant chord whose root is a *tritone* (or ♭5) away—a distance of three whole steps ("tri" is the Greek word for "three"). For example, you can substitute a G7 chord with a D♭7 (or some other dominant) chord since D♭ is a tritone away from G. Finding voicings that work is the key.

This works because when you compare the spelling of both chords, a D♭7 looks and sounds like a G7♭5♭9 without a root. What you are really doing is adding some altered tones to the original chord and dropping the root.

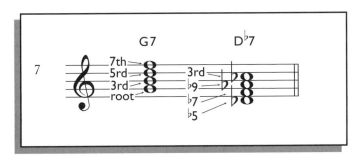

Besides giving you another harmonic perspective, this technique gives you a nice chromatic bass line in the context of the common ii-V7-I progression:

	ii	V7	I
Standard:	Dmin7	G7	CMaj9
With a tritone substitution:	Dmin7	D♭9	CMaj9

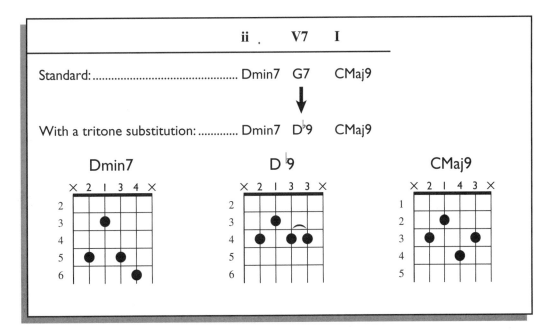

Yet another way to think about this is to look at the circle of 5ths—all the tritone substitutions are directly across the circle from each other.

APPROACH CHORDS

This is a great way to dress up your harmonies. You can approach any chord with a dominant chord (altered or otherwise) whose root is a half step away. The approach can be from above or below. Experiment and find tasteful ways to do this.

Here is an unadorned, basic chord progression:

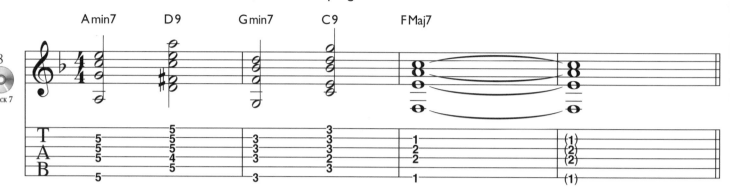

Here it is again with approach chords (approach chords are marked with asterisks):

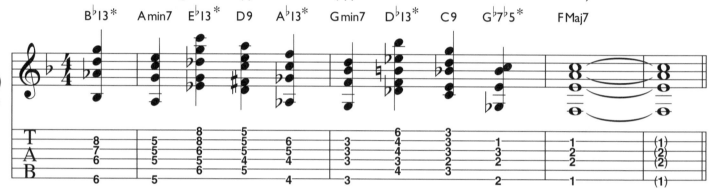

Besides being a nice thing to do while comping, you can also include these moves while harmonizing a melody. Here is our progression again, without approach chords, with a melody:

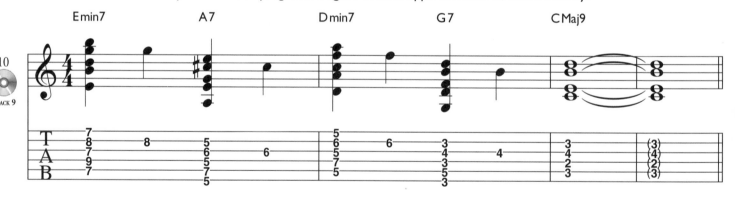

Here is the melody and progression again, this time harmonized with approach chords:

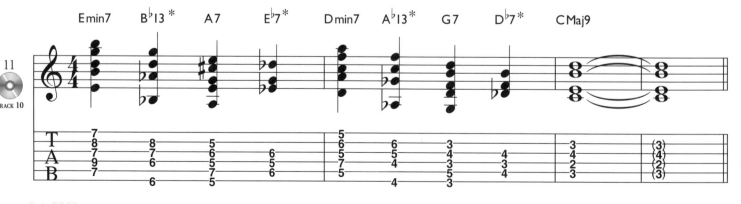

JAZZ
SKILLS

This section will get you started with this wonderful comping technique. The idea is to *comp* (accompany) with chords and play a *walking bass line* at the same time.

A walking bass line is one that moves mostly by step, using *passing tones* (tones from the scale of the key or chord of the moment). Sometimes, *chromatic passing tones* (tones that do not belong to the scale of the key or chord) are included.

When executed well, the effect of comping with chords and a walking bass line simultaneously is that of two instruments playing at once. To get a more complete picture, be sure to check out Chapter 5 in *Mastering Jazz Guitar: Chord/Melody*.

STEP 1:
Learn and memorize these four shapes for Cmin7 chords:

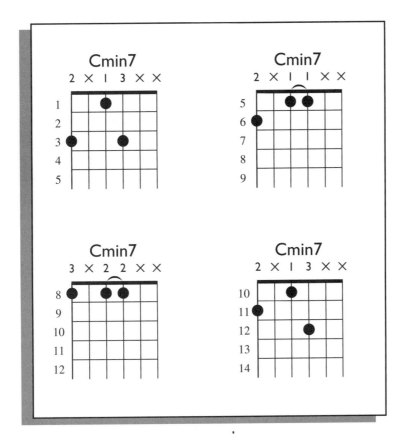

The following steps will lead you to a Cmin7 *vamp*. A vamp is an accompaniment figure or pattern that is repeated. It is often used as an introduction and is repeated until all the performers are ready to continue.

STEP 2:

Think like a bass player. The bass line needs to move between the tones of one chord to the tones of the next chord. The simplest way is to move between chord tones scalewise—by step using the notes of the scale of the key. Another way is to approach the chord tone from a step above or a step below. Sometimes bass lines even skip into a chord tone from a *tritone* (♭5) away.

Here is a summary of ways bass players move between chord tones in walking bass lines:

1. Scalewise.
2. From a half step below.
3. From a half step above.
4. From a whole step above.
5. From a whole step below.
6. From a ♭5 away.

You must be conscious of the key you are in. There may be an approach to some chords that will not fit in the key. If treated with taste, these approaches can sound great. Experiment.

Practice playing in 4/4 time and begin with the "half step below" approach. Travel up the fingerboard like this:

Play a chord.
Play a bass note one half step below the root of the next chord.
Play the next chord.
Play a bass note one half step below the root of the next chord.
Play the next chord.
Etc.

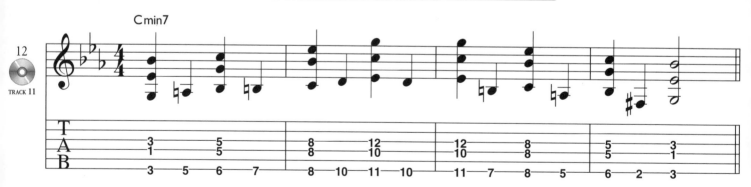

Continue alternating this way between bass note, chord, bass note, chord, etc.—up and down the entire neck. Practice this way using all of the approaches listed above. Be sure to keep a steady rhythm. For now, just play a steady stream of quarter notes at a tempo that feels comfortable. Later, you will try to think and play faster.

STEP 3:

Experiment with the right hand. You have three basic options for sounding the bass notes and chords:

1. Striking the chord and bass note simultaneously as in example 12 on page 32.
2. Striking the bass note just a little ahead of the rest of the chord:

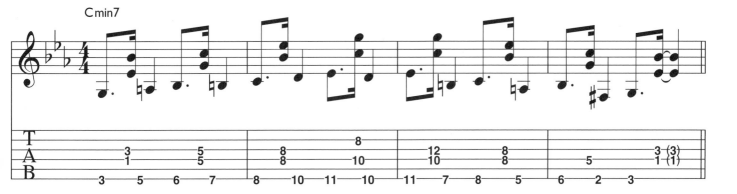

3. Striking the chord just a little ahead of the bass note:

Of course, a real playing situation would include all three approaches.

STEP 4:

Transpose all these ideas, as demonstrated in examples 12–14, to all twelve keys so that you have complete flexibility in this technique.

STEP 5:

Learn voicings for dominant and major chords and apply all the previous information to them. Here are some starter voicings.

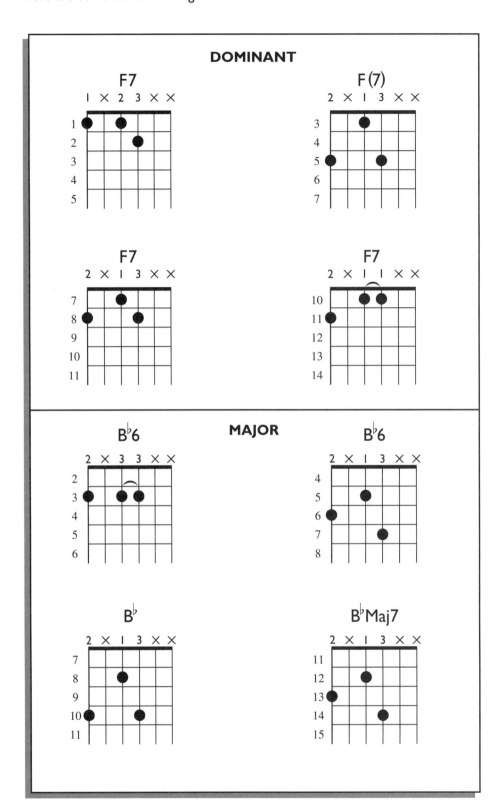

STEP 6:

Work out lots of ii-V7-I chord patterns using all of the techniques described above. Here are some samples:

STEP 7:

Practice this technique comping the changes to tunes from the standard jazz repertoire.

REALITY CHECK

This process should take you months to go through and there will always be more to know. Getting started is always the hardest part, but it really does get easier as you progress. The results are well worth the effort!

SECTION II — IMPROVISING

In this section, we'll start by learning some scales and arpeggios and EXPLORE ways to make music with them. It should be stressed that simply knowing this information will not make you a great improviser. What you really need to do is *listen*. Listen to a lot of improvised music and try to hear how others use this information. These are just the building blocks—what you do with them is the real issue.

THE MAJOR SCALE

Let's look at six fingerings for the major scale. There are many other fingerings, but I prefer these because they allow you to play in almost any key—anywhere on the fingerboard—easily. Here they are in the key of G:

ROOTS ON THE 6TH STRING

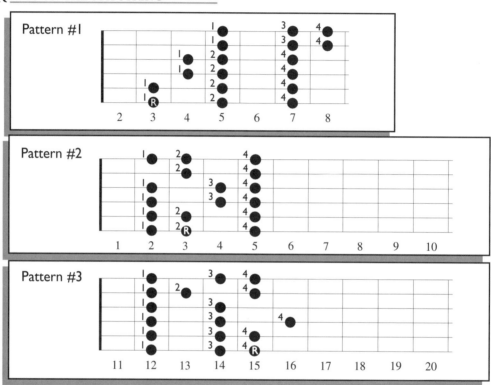

ROOTS ON THE 5TH STRING

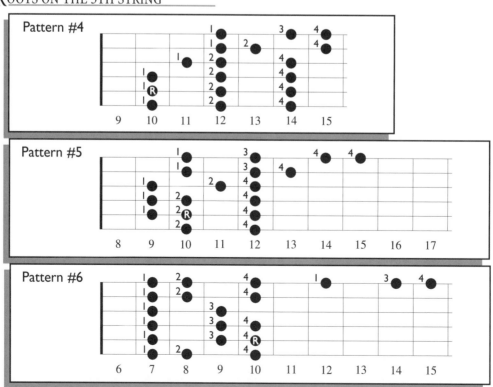

The advantage that these fingerings have is that no matter what *position* you are in, you can play in eleven different keys with minimal shifting. (Let's define a position as being a six-fret area.) This is very useful when you have to improvise over a chord progression that moves rapidly through many key centers. For example, the following diagrams show the roots of all the keys you can play in using these scale patterns around the 4th and 9th positions.

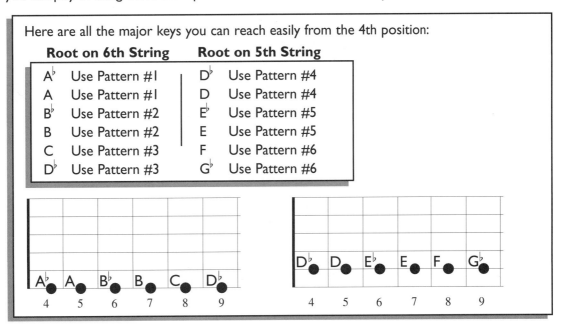

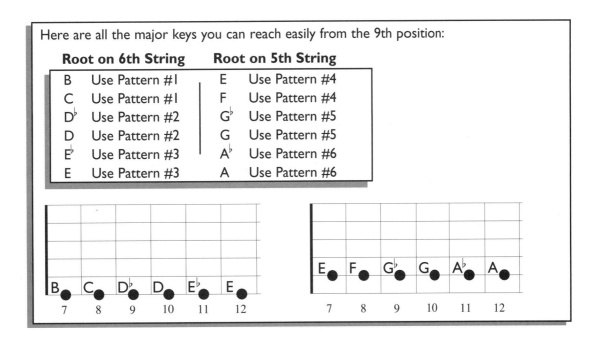

The major scale is a good starting point for improvisation because it can be used in so many ways over so many types of chords and chord progressions.

There are seven chords that are produced by harmonizing the major scale (see page 12). For example, in the key of G, the diatonic chords are: GMaj7, Amin7, Bmin7, CMaj7, D7, Emin7 and F#min7♭5.

You can use the G Major scale to improvise over any of those chords. Some notes in the scale will sound better than others over a given chord but overall, you can play the major scale freely over a progression that consists of diatonic chords.

Practice improvising over this chord progression using a G Major scale. Either play along with the CD that is available for this book, record the chord progression yourself or get a friend to play the chords.

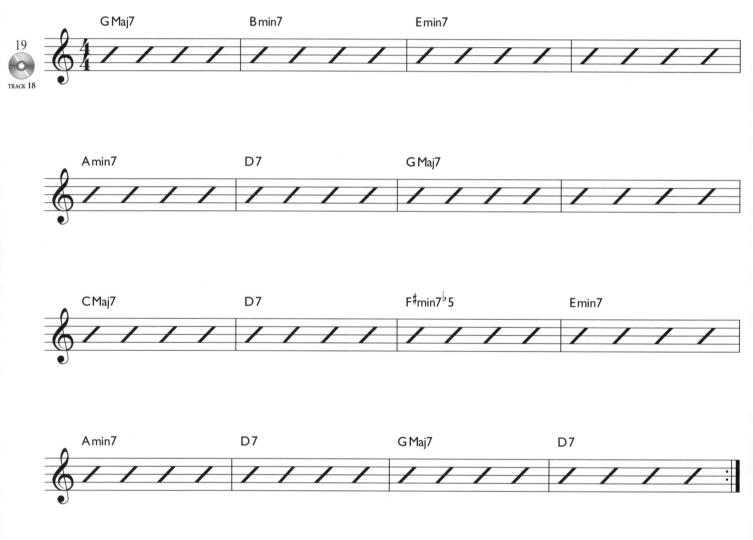

This concept is a little larger than it seems at first. Very few jazz chord progressions consist of only diatonic chords, but with a slight change in perspective, you can use this information in those situations as well. The following information should get you up and running but this is a huge topic. You should investigate it further. Check out *The Complete Jazz Guitar Method* or *The Guitar Mode Encyclopedia*.

In the *derivative approach,* you look at a chord and decide to use a major scale from which it was produced. When you see a Dmin7 chord, you think: Dmin7 is the ii chord of C, the iii chord of B♭ and the vi chord of F. This means that you can use the C, B♭ or F Major scales to improvise. They will each produce a unique sound, but some choices will be more appropriate than others depending upon the context. Obviously, the chord tones would be accented while improvising.

If you are familiar with the modes of the major scale, it is important for you to note that what you are actually doing in the derivative approach is thinking modally. For example, if you are playing the C Major scale because you are playing over a Dmin7 chord (as described in the paragraph above), and are stressing the chord tones (D, F, A, C), you are playing the D Dorian mode!

QUICK REVIEW OF THE MODES OF THE MAJOR SCALE:

If you play a major scale starting and ending on the 1st degree, you are playing the Ionian mode.

2nd	Dorian
3rd	Phrygian
4th	Lydian
5th	Mixolydian
6th	Aeolian
7th	Locrian

This chart shows some examples of derivative thinking. And, for those of you who are knowledgeable about the modes, it shows what mode is being generated by thinking this way.

Chord	Scale Choice	Modal Sound
GMaj7	G Major (G Maj7 is the I chord)	G Ionian
	D Major (GMaj7 is the IV chord)	G Lydian
Fmin7	E♭ Major (Fmin7 is the ii chord)	F Dorian
	D♭ Major (Fmin7 is the iii chord)	F Phrygian
	A♭ Major (Fmin7 is the vi chord)	F Aeolian
A7	D Major (A7 is the V7 chord)	A Mixolydian
Dmin7♭5	E♭ Major (Dmin7♭5 is the vii chord)	D Locrian

The following examples show a few possibilities.

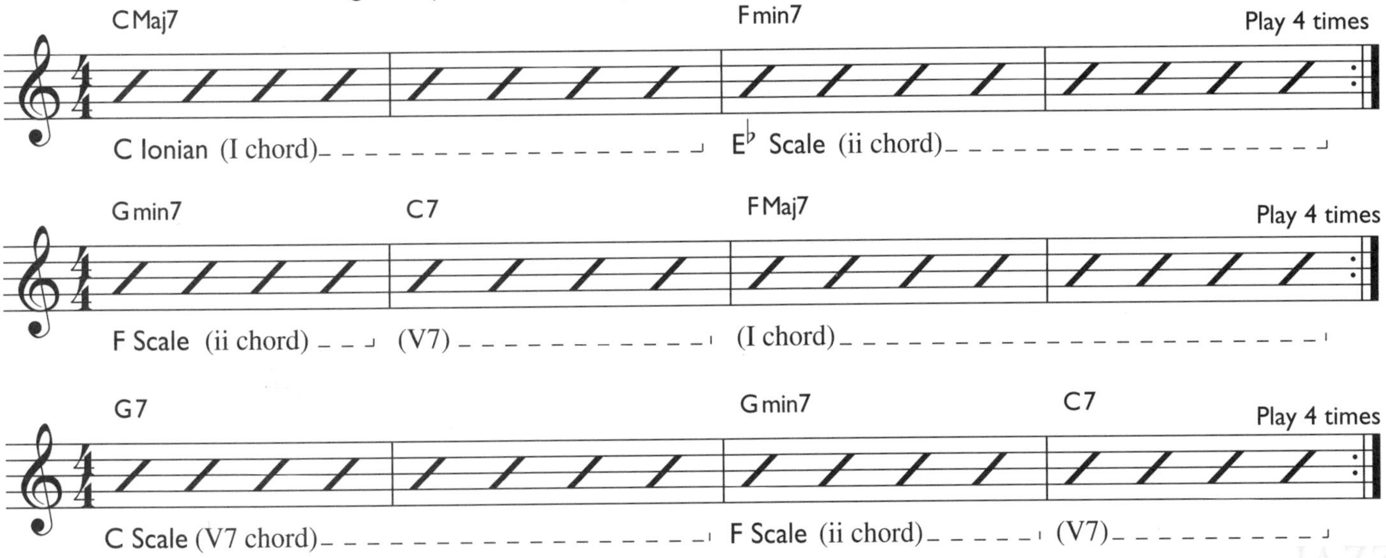

CMaj7 / Fmin7 — Play 4 times
C Ionian (I chord) — E♭ Scale (ii chord)

Gmin7 / C7 / FMaj7 — Play 4 times
F Scale (ii chord) — (V7) — (I chord)

G7 / Gmin7 / C7 — Play 4 times
C Scale (V7 chord) — F Scale (ii chord) — (V7)

In order to put this concept to use, you need to know:

A. The major scales on the guitar and by recitation.
B. The chords in each major scale and their position in the key.

Again, this is actually modal thinking. When you are using that C Major scale over the Dmin7 chord you are playing a D Dorian mode (going from D to D, using the notes of the C Major scale.)

THE PARALLEL APPROACH

Some players prefer learning separate fingerings for each mode. This is called the *parallel approach*. In other words, when improvising over a D7 chord, some players will use a D Mixolydian mode fingering. Of course, this would be the same thing as playing a G Major scale over the D7. It's a matter of preference.

Here are fingerings for each mode in the C Major scale (see page 36 for Ionian fingerings):

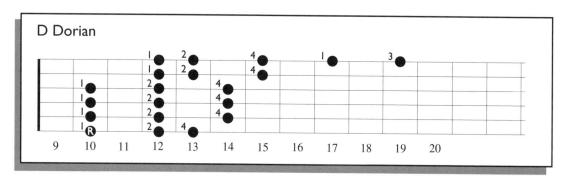

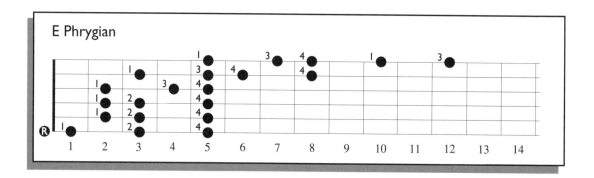

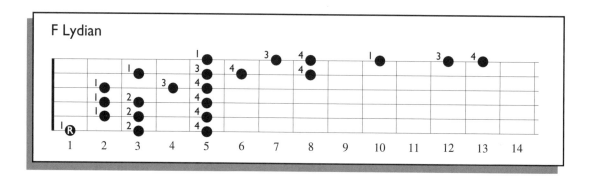

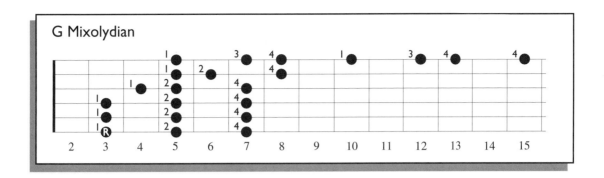

G Mixolydian

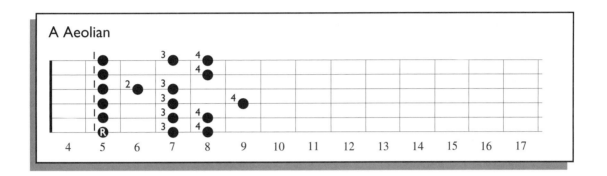

A Aeolian

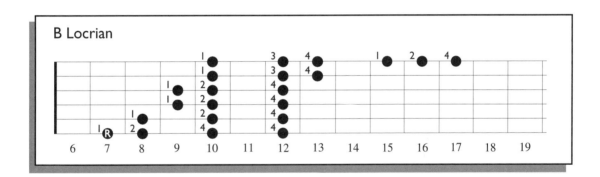

B Locrian

There are many types of minor scales. The following is an overview of the most basic minor scales you need to know.

THE NATURAL MINOR SCALE

The *natural minor scale* is the basic minor scale. It comes from the 6th degree of any major scale. Using a C Major scale, we see that the 6th degree is A. The A Natural Minor scale is built by starting on A and proceeding through the notes of the C Major scale until A is reached again. The G Natural Minor scale would travel from G to G using the notes of a B♭ Major scale, etc. The two scales share a common key signature. The key signature for B♭ Major is the same as the key signature for G Minor. This is known as the *relative minor* relationship. G Minor is the relative minor to B♭ Major; A Minor is the relative minor to C Major, etc. The Aeolian mode (see page 39) is another name for the natural minor scale.

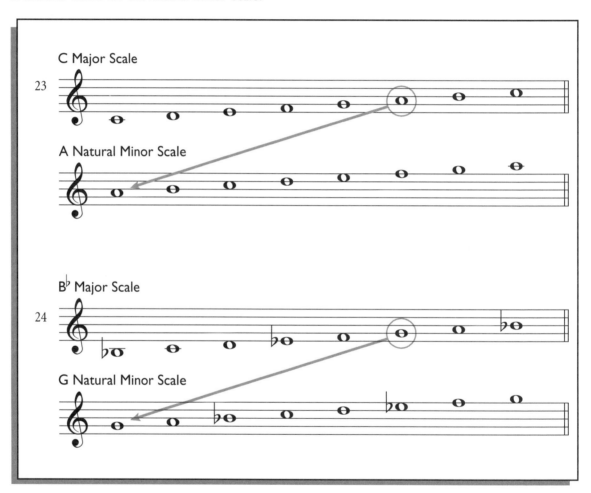

FINGERINGS FOR A NATURAL MINOR

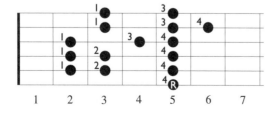
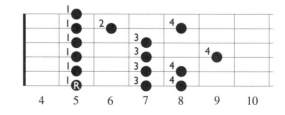

THE HARMONIC MINOR SCALE

Think of the *harmonic minor scale* as a natural minor scale with a raised 7th degree. For an in depth study of the scale and its modes, check out the *Guitar Mode Encyclopedia*.

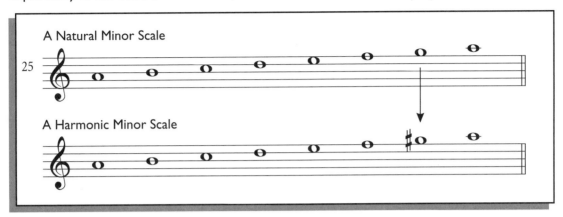

As with the major scale, creating modes will give you even more sounds to work with as an improviser. Below is a list of modes generated by the harmonic minor scale and the kinds of chords they work with. As with the modes of the major scale, you can think in terms of a parallel approach or a derivative approach. The modes in this diagram are all derived from A Harmonic Minor.

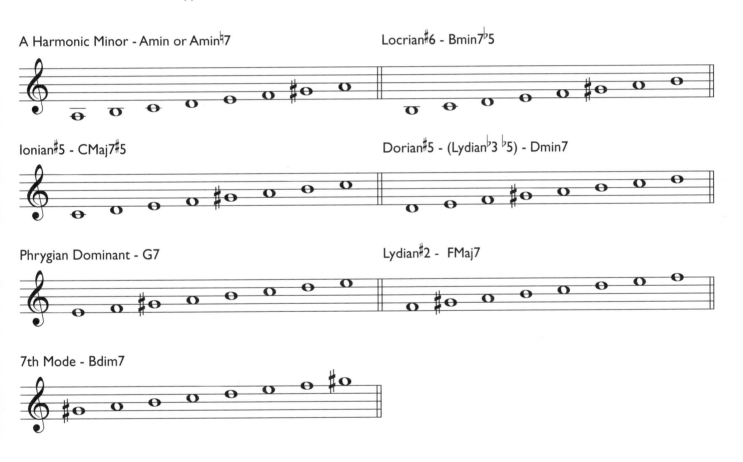

FINGERINGS FOR A HARMONIC MINOR

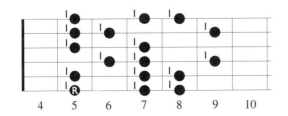

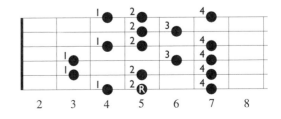

The Melodic Minor Scale—Jazz Minor

Raise both the 6th and 7th degrees of a natural minor scale and you have a *melodic minor scale.*

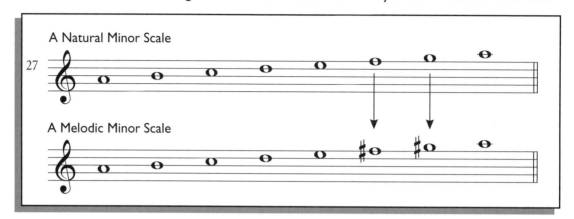

Traditionally, the raised notes occur in the ascending scale only. The descending scale returns to the natural minor scale.

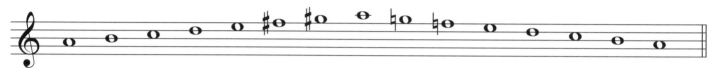

This, however, doesn't do us much good while improvising so we apply the raised notes in both the ascending and descending scale—some players call this version the *jazz minor scale.*

FINGERINGS FOR THE A MELODIC (JAZZ) MINOR

An even easier approach is to lower the 3rd of a major scale:

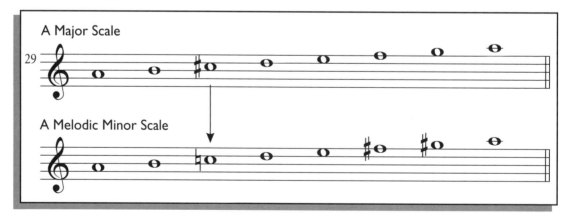

Again, you can create modes from the melodic minor and of course, they work well over the corresponding chords with either a derivative or parallel approach.

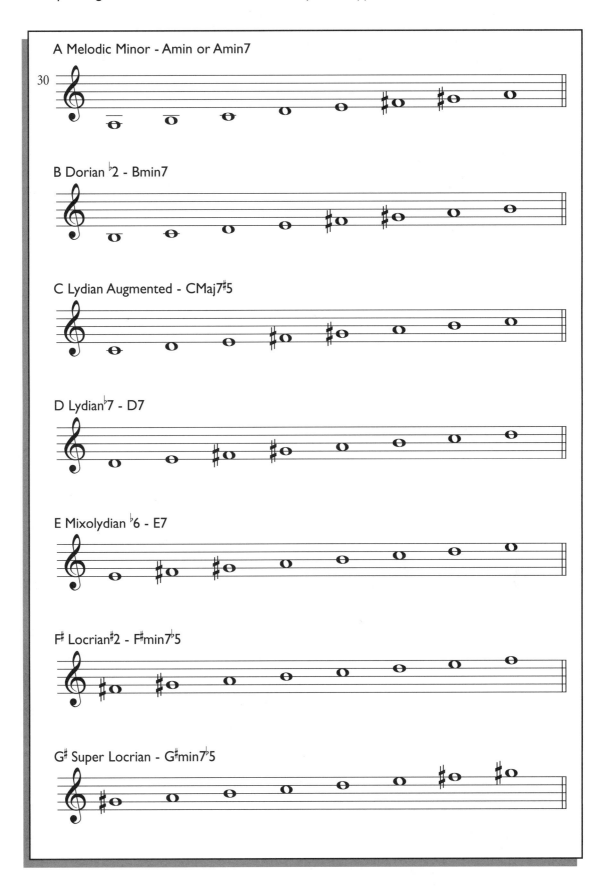

So many players use these scales exclusively that it's difficult to believe that a jazz skills student would still need to learn what they are about. Yet it seems like many jazz students *do* need to brush-up on some of this material.

THE MAJOR PENTATONIC SCALE

The *major pentatonic scale* is really a major scale without the 4th and 7th degrees. As such, you can use it in exactly the same way as a major scale. If you have been playing pop music for any length of time, you probably have a collection of licks and other ideas using pentatonic scales. Go ahead—try them in jazz tunes. They work and will tend to add a different dimension to your solos. For example, if you are used to playing major scale ideas over ii-V7-I progressions using the major scale of the I chord, try the major pentatonic scale based on the I chord for a switch.

C MAJOR PENTATONIC FINGERINGS

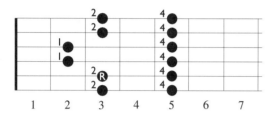
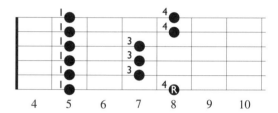

THE MINOR PENTATONIC SCALE

The *minor pentatonic scale* is one of the first scales most people learn. It is used widely in rock, pop and country music—and you can sound pretty good almost immediately. While the major pentatonic scale will give you sweet major sounds, the minor pentatonic scale will give you a bluesier edge. Use it over minor and unaltered dominant chords.

Any pentatonic scale fingering can be both major or minor depending on what you perceive the root to be. This relationship works the same way as relative major and minor keys. In other words, C Major Pentatonic = A Minor Pentatonic; F Major Pentatonic = D Minor Pentatonic, etc.

C MINOR PENTATONIC FINGERINGS

Notice that these are exactly the same fingerings as the C Major Pentatonic fingerings above. Only the root has changed.

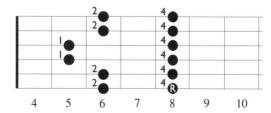
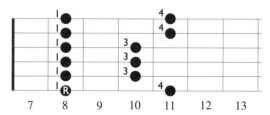

The *blues scale* is often thought of as a minor pentatonic scale with the ♭5 added. It's a familiar but beautiful sound. You can add this tone to the major pentatonic scale as well. Of course in a major context, you've added the ♭3. Experiment with this over major chord progressions.

A BLUES SCALE FINGERINGS

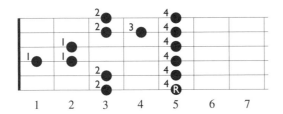

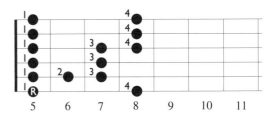

A MAJOR PENTATONIC WITH AN ADDED ♭3 FINGERINGS

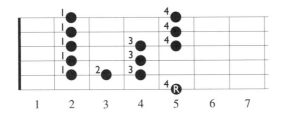

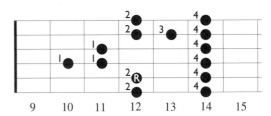

Try using your familiar pentatonic fingerings in different ways:

For major chords:	Use a major pentatonic scale starting from the root, 5th or 9th of the chord.
For minor chords:	Use a minor pentatonic scale starting from the root, 5th or 9th of the chord.
For dominant sus4 chords (1-4-5-♭7):	Use a major pentatonic starting on the root or ♭7 of the chord.
For altered dominant 7 chords:	Use a major pentatonic scale starting from the ♭5 over chords with altered 5ths and 9ths.

See my *Guitar Chord & Scale Finder* for more interesting uses for pentatonic scales.

There are so many scales to use over altered dominant chords that it is easy to be overwhelmed. In truth, it's not how much you know that makes you a good improviser but how you *use* what you do know.

There are three essential scales to use over altered chords. The *diminished scale* is the first.

THE DIMINISHED SCALE

The diminished scale is a *symmetrical scale*. In other words, its design is a symmetrical pattern of whole steps and half steps. The formula is whole - half - whole - half -whole - half - whole, etc.

C Diminished Scale

Start the diminished scale one half step above the root of the altered dominant chord you are improvising over. In other words, you could use an A♭ Diminished scale over an altered G7 chord.

Almost all possible alterations (see page 16) are included in this scale. Below is the A♭ Diminished scale. Beneath each tone is the note's relationship to a G7 chord.

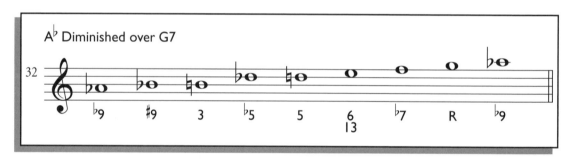

As you can see, this scale would sound fine over any G7 with a ♭5, ♯9 or ♭9 (or any combination of these). The only altered tone which would not be reflected in the scale is the ♯5.

In the case of the following progression, Gmin7–C7♯5–FMaj7, you could use the F Major scale over the Gmin7 and the FMaj7. Over the C7♭5, a D♭ Diminished scale would work very well.

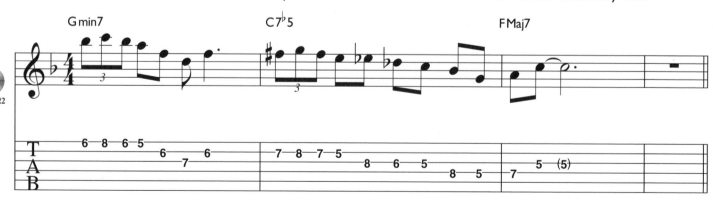

NOTE: In this book, as in most jazz contexts, it is safe to assume that the eighth notes should be swung. "Swing 8ths" are performed by holding the first eighth in each pair longer than its written value. The second eighth is played late, and shorter. The swing rhythm sounds like an eighth-note triplet with the first two eighths tied.

Because the diminished scale is a symmetrical scale, any fingering for the diminished scale can be moved up or down minor 3rds and it will include the same notes—very convenient!

A DIMINISHED SCALE FINGERINGS

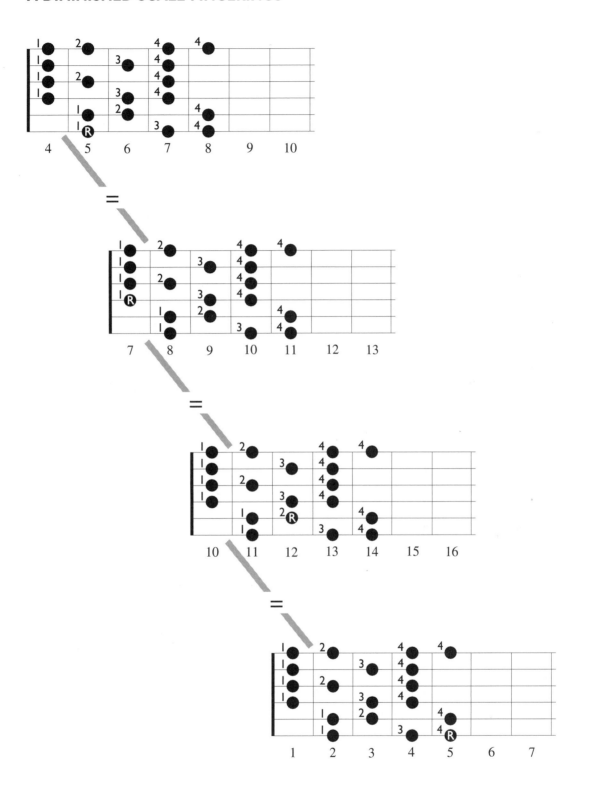

Some players prefer to think of the diminished scale's formula as half–whole–half–whole–half–whole, etc. In this case, you would start the scale from the root of the altered dominant scale instead. All the above considerations would still hold true.

There are really only two *whole tone scales*. Because of the arrangement of whole steps, whole tone scales beginning from every other note on the chromatic scale contain identical tones.

When improvising, start the whole tone scale from the root of the dominant chord. This is what we get when we superimpose a G Whole Tone scale over a G7 chord:

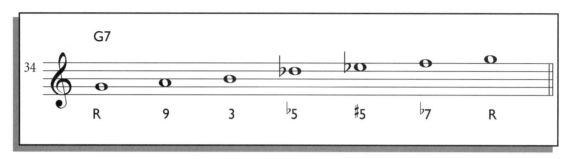

The whole tone scale works well over dominant chords with raised or lowered 5ths.

Here is a ii-V7-I progression in C using a G Whole Tone scale over G7♭5:

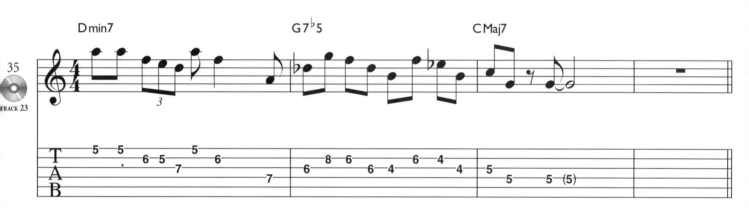

G WHOLE TONE SCALE FINGERINGS

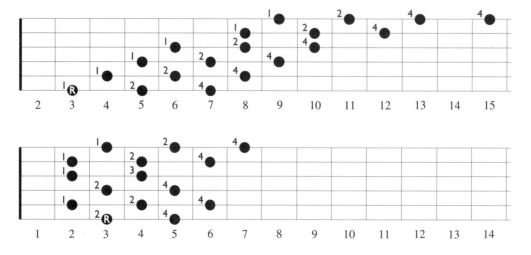

This box shape comes in handy when you want to use whole tone sounds. The notes in this shape, played in any order and then moved around in whole steps, will give you colorful whole tone sounds. Just start from any chord tone!

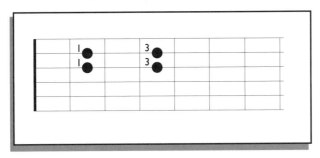

Here are two examples of this shape in use:

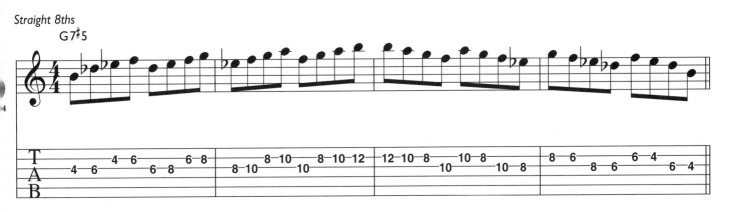

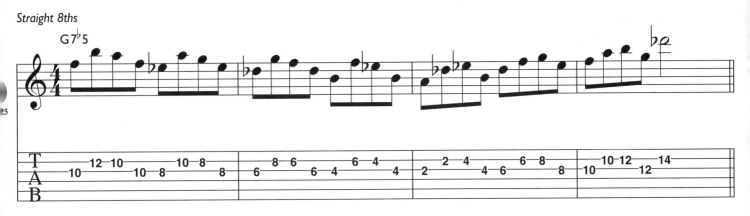

The *Super Locrian scale* goes by many names. You will also see this called the *altered dominant scale* or the *diminished whole tone scale*. It is undoubtedly the most usable of the altered scales because it contains the ♭5, ♯5, ♭9 and ♯9. It is the 7th mode of the melodic minor scale. Many jazz players create these sounds by playing a melodic minor scale one half step above the root of the altered dominant chord. I think it is easier and a little more practical to think of it as a separate scale.

Here is the G Super Locrian scale and its relationship to a G7 chord:

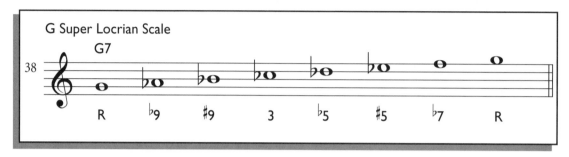

G SUPER LOCRIAN FINGERINGS

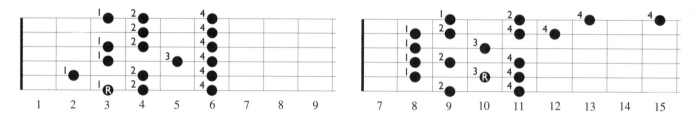

Here is the Super Locrian scale in use over a ii-V7-I progression:

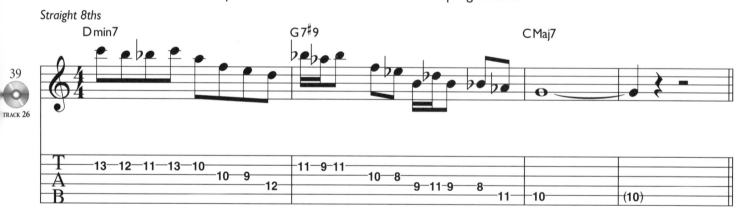

One way to capture the flavor of any altered chord in your solos is to start your phrase from the highest altered tone in the chord (for example, the ♯9 in a ♭5♯9 chord), and then proceed to the altered scale of your choice.

ARPEGGIOS

One sure sign of proficiency as an improviser is the ability to *spell out the changes*. Your improvised lines should reflect the chord changes as accurately as possible. At the most advanced level, this means echoing not only the chord changes, but the alterations in the chords as well.

At a more basic level, you need to learn to accent the chord tones within the scales. The study of *arpeggios* will give you the ammunition you need in order to do this. This chapter will give you a great start.

Arpeggios are the notes in a chord played consecutively rather than simultaneously. In the system shown here, you will learn all the arpeggios for the seven diatonic chords within a particular major scale fingering.

Here is the major scale fingering that the arpeggios will be based on:

THE C MAJOR SCALE

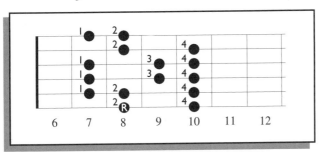

Below are the diatonic arpeggios within this scale. Chord examples are included. Once you have learned the arpeggio shapes, practice them by playing the chord, then the arpeggio and then the chord one more time. This way, you will learn to associate the arpeggio with the chord itself.

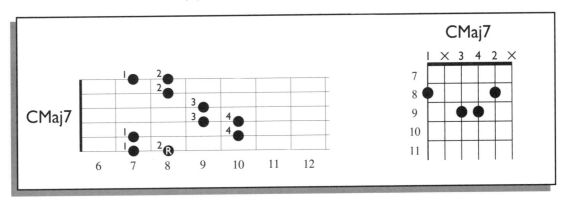

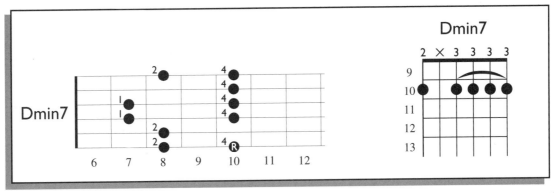

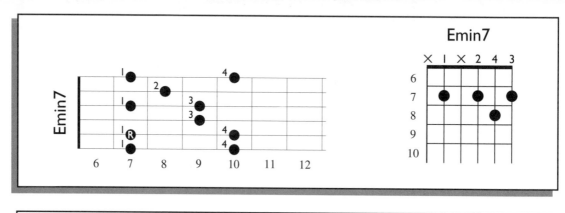

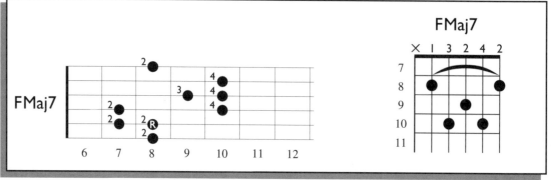

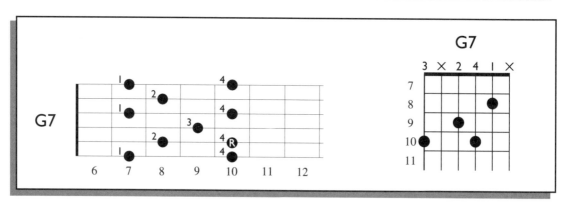

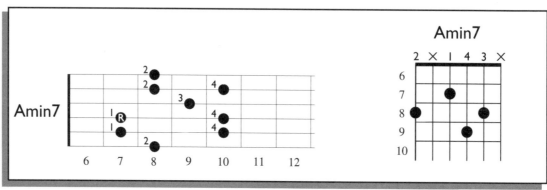

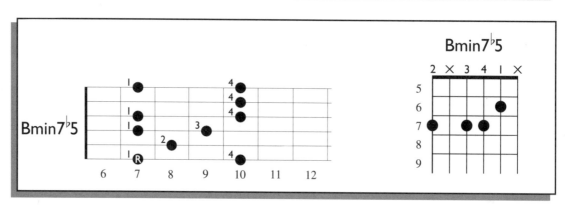

Eventually, you should try to learn a set of diatonic arpeggios for every major scale fingering you know.

The first step in learning to spell out changes is learning your arpeggios. If you have memorized the previous set, then it is time to move on.

Many of us begin improvising by randomly running up and down the scales that will work over a particular chord progression. Now, you should start your improvised lines with chord tones. Start your phrases on roots, 3rds, 5ths and 7ths of the chords and still use the major scale to improvise—it's just the first note of each phrase that will be a chord tone. Try to start with 3rds and 7ths often, because of their defining role in all chords (these tones define the quality of the chord—whether they are major, minor or dominant). Try to start on a chord tone every time the chord changes in the progression.

This may seem a little rigid at first. After some experience with this technique, you will know when it is necessary and when it is not.

Here are some examples of lines that start on the various chord tones:

NEIGHBOR TONES

Once you have a handle on starting your lines from a chord tone, the next step is learning to use *neighbor tones*. These are notes that an improviser uses to approach *targeted* chord tones. There are many notes that can be considered neighbor tones, but for now we'll stick to notes that are either a half step or a whole step above or below the chord tone. The chord tone will fall on the first beat of each measure, so you'll need to "plan ahead" to make sure your neighbor tones fall on either beat 4, or on the second half of beat 4 of the previous measure.

I = Whole step
½ = Half step

Here are some neighbor tone examples:

NEIGHBOR TONES AROUND CHORD SHAPES

You can also apply the neighbor tone idea to chord shapes. If you are improvising over this chord:

Amin7

You will consider the gray notes your neighbor tones:

Amin7

You can then come up with lines like these (chord tones are circled the first time they appear):

Amin7

Straight 8ths
E7#9

Straight 8ths
FMaj7

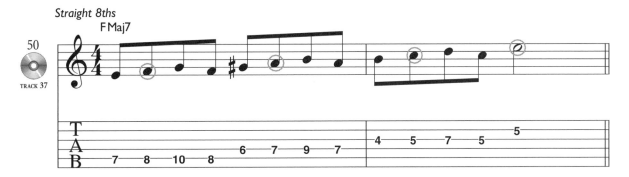

Altered clusters are small groupings of notes that will help you reflect altered tones in your solos. There are eight different kinds of altered clusters: clusters will help you learn to recognize these sounds when you hear them.

7♭5	7♭5♭9
7♯5	7♯5♯9
7♭9	7♭5♯9
7♯9	7♯5♭9

Below, there are five clusters shown over the fingerboard for each one. Each cluster has a root, 3rd and ♭7 in addition to whatever altered tone(s) there may be (♭5, ♯5, ♭9, ♯9). The natural 5th is also added to those clusters in which there is no altered 5th. The altered clusters give you places all over the fingerboard to target the essential tones of any altered chord. Practicing these clusters will help you learn to recognize these sounds when you hear them.

C7♭5

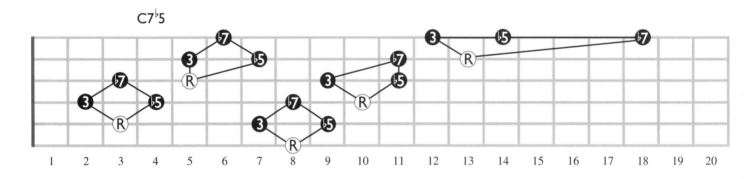

C7♯5

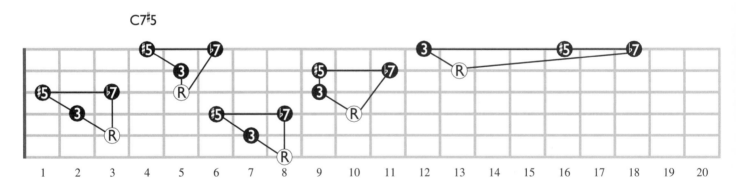

C7♭9

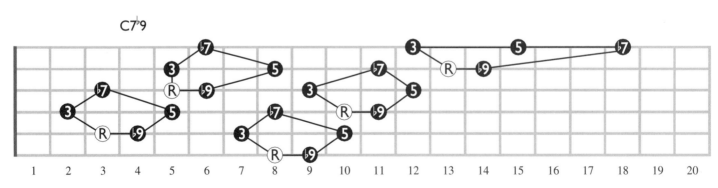

JAZZ
SKILLS

C7#9

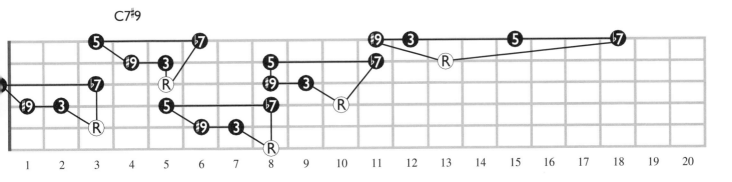

C7♭5♭9

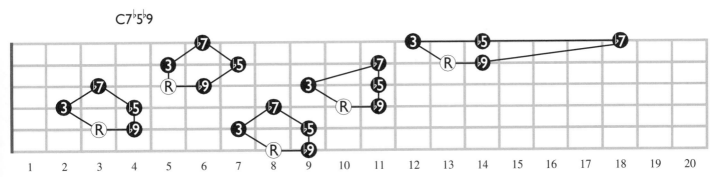

C7#5♯9

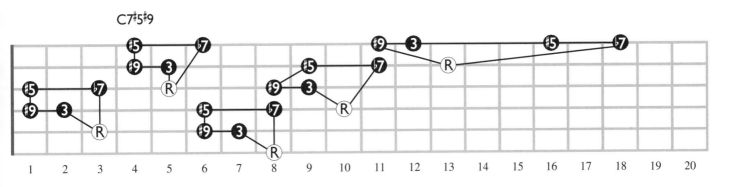

C7#5♭9

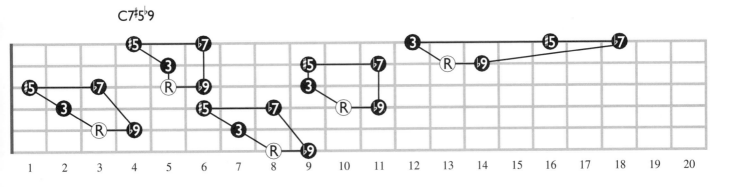

C7♭5#9

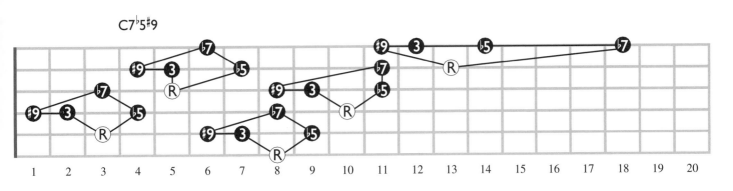

Playing "*outside*" means to temporarily play outside of the key. This creates *tension* (*dissonance*, or clashing sounds) in the solo and adds interest to the overall contour. You can't just decide to play outside whenever you want—periods of tension must be followed by periods of *release* (*consonance*, in harmony). The tasteful use of outside devices takes time to develop. You have to approach them with confidence. Playing outside with a tentative feeling only sounds wrong. Strong outside playing should be followed by a strong resolution back to the key center. The following are a few devices that work well.

SYMMETRICAL MOVES

One way to get an outside sound is to take a *motive* (a short phrase that is repeated) and move it around the fingerboard in symmetrical intervals—half steps, minor 3rds, chromatically, etc. The listener's ear will "track" the symmetry more than the phrase's relationship to the harmony. When you are ready to resolve, land on a chord tone.

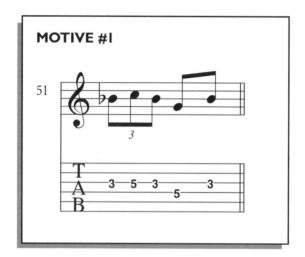

In this example, the motive moves up *chromatically* (by half step). Notice how it finally comes to rest on a chord tone, thus releasing the tension.

In this example, the motive moves up and then down in minor 3rds.

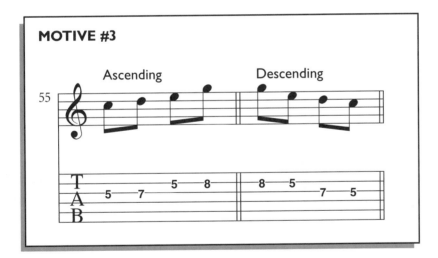

This time, the motive alternates ascending and descending, up a minor 3rd and then down one half step.

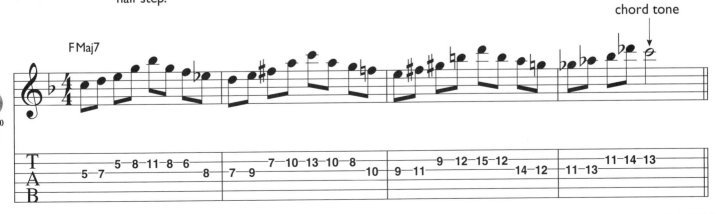

MOVING UP OR DOWN A HALF STEP

This is fairly easy to accomplish. The trick is to pick just the precise moment to execute the idea. Stay out of key just long enough to create a surprise—then resolve back to the original key. Like all of these devices, use it sparingly.

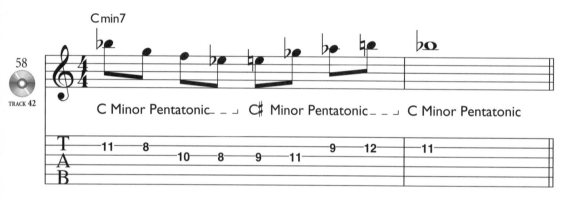

MELODIC PATTERNS BASED AROUND ARPEGGIO SHAPES

With this device, play a motive starting from each tone in an arpeggio's fingering. Your motive does not have to suggest any key at all. When you start each phrase from a chord tone, you will find there are enough *inside* sounds (notes from within the key) being played to "stay in touch" with the key center. The other notes in the pattern will give you the outside edge you are looking for.

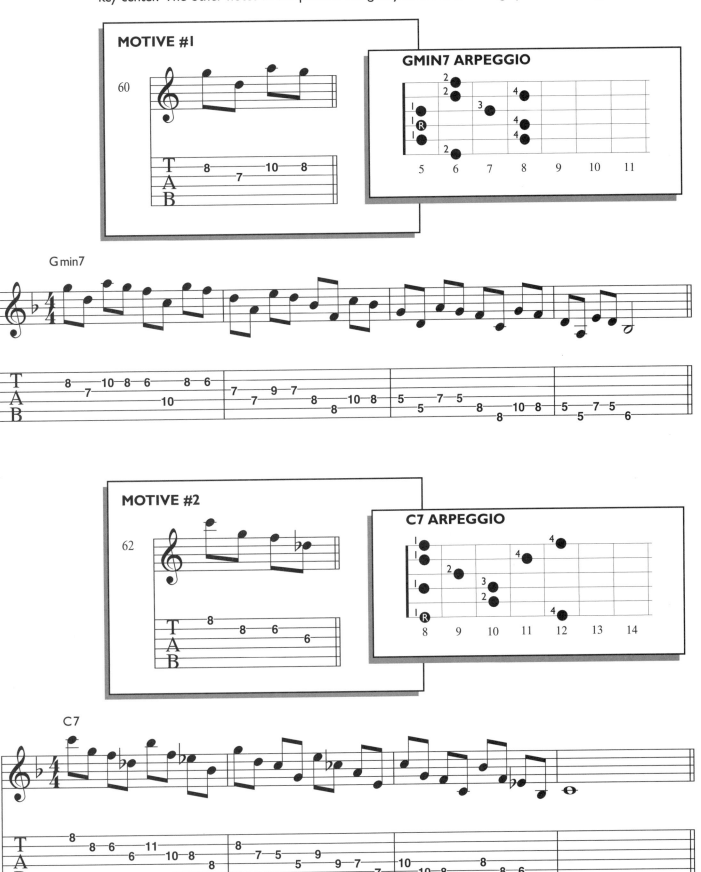

SECTION III — READING

The art of reading music on guitar is a huge topic. In this book we will concentrate on the areas that students ask about the most.

Why do I need to read music?

Being able to read is part of the total package of being a competent musician. Sure, there have been many great players who couldn't read, but they didn't become great *because* they couldn't read. Not knowing how to read is like being illiterate. It's like being able to speak English but not being able to read or write it. If you can't read, you'll miss out on a lot of the music that has been written through the centuries. If you read well, you'll learn tunes more quickly. Examples in books like this one will become easier to learn, too.

We're not talking about becoming an ace sight-reader here. Sight-reading refers to the ability to play something almost perfectly by the first or second read-through—with all the *dynamics* (signs indicating the degree of loudness and softness) and phrasing in place, up to tempo and played with feeling. In reality, very few of us need to become *that* good. For most of us, being able to read through a piece of music at a moderate tempo accurately and comfortably is good enough. Reading is a mechanical skill, and you can become quite good. It is mostly a matter of desire and practice.

What is the best system for reading on the guitar?

There probably is no "best" system. People use what works for them and there are many different ways to think about reading.

At first, there are two main considerations—note identification and reading rhythm. We will cover both of these areas in the following pages.

This book assumes that you can already read in the first position (you understand about the notes and the staff, time signatures, key signatures, the basic note values and you know the names of notes on the first five frets). If you are not yet a reading musician and you have been relying solely on the tablature and diagrams to use this book, you should pick up a beginning reading method and work your way through it. You can continue to work through the rest of this book as you have thus far.

I prefer a system that uses the six major scale fingerings shown earlier in the book. If a piece of music you are going to read is in the key of F Major, you have six fingerings of an F Major scale to choose from. They cover the entire range of the guitar. As with the improvising aspect of the scales, you can read in eleven keys in any six-fret position.

The following exercises are examples of how you can practice your note reading. They contain only quarter notes. These exercises are in a few different keys. There are a lot of accidentals in some examples, but treat them as departures from the scale of the key indicated in the key signatures. Practice each exercise in one fingering until it becomes easy. Then practice it again using one of the other scale fingerings you know and so, on until you have read in all the fingerings that are practical for the exercise. Obviously, if there are a lot of notes that fall on the lower ledger lines, you won't want to use a fingering that stays in the upper range of the fingerboard, or vice versa. It is common, however, to shift to a few different positions during the same piece to accommodate parts of songs that travel to higher or lower octaves. Whenever you read something, experiment with the different scale fingerings first to find the best position(s). Experiment with reading the following examples. Try to find the most practical fingerings for each.

(Continued on page 67)

Reading rhythm is a problem area for musicians. It is a lot like reading words. When you first learned to read, you needed to "sound out" all the letters to come up with the word. After a while, you simply recognized the word every time you saw it. As time went on, you were able to recognize more and more words until you could read just about anything. Learning to read rhythms is similar. At first, you count out every part of a measure. After a while, you start to notice that a lot of the same figures are used over and over again. You recognize the figure and you know what it sounds like. You eventually just play the rhythm when you see it. This takes a little time.

Use any note for the following exercises. Play them with a metronome at different tempos and with different feels. If you have a drum machine to practice with, these studies become a little more fun.

68
TRACK 50

After you have perfected all these exercises, read the rhythms from any piece of music you have—a fake book, sheet music…anything. Don't worry about the melody for now; just play the rhythmic figures on a single note.

PUTTING IT ALL TOGETHER

When you have gained some confidence finding the notes and reading rhythmic figures, try putting it all together. Here are some general tips:

- Always check the key signature and time signature before you begin to read any tune.

- Look at the range of the tune. Find the highest note and the lowest. This will suggest an appropriate scale fingering or position.

- Study the tune rhythmically. Most players mark their music in places they may find difficult. Always keep a pencil handy.

- Find all repeats, *Da Capos, Dal Segnos, Codas*, and so on ahead of time. Know the road map! If these terms are unfamiliar to you, get a good reading method and/or music dictionary. Here is a quick review:

Coda	Ending section. Marked $\oplus$.
D. C. al Fine	(*Da Capo al Fine*) Go back to beginning and play until the *Fine* (end).
D. C. al Coda	(*Da Capo al Coda*) Go back to beginning and play to the *Coda* sign $\oplus$. Then skip to the end and play the *Coda* section.
D. S. al Coda	(*Dal Segno al Coda*) Go back to the sign 𝄋 and play to the *Coda* sign $\oplus$. Then skip to the end and play the *Coda* section.
D. S. al Fine	(*Dal Segno al Fine*) Go back to sign 𝄋 and play until the *Fine* (end).

- Find any *modulations* (changes of key) and time signature changes ahead of time.

- Check for dynamic markings.

- Keep your eye moving across the page from left to right. Don't look back to see if you've missed a note. You will miss many more notes coming up if you keep checking previous measures.

- Play with confidence and assume you're hitting the right notes. Try to take in as many notes as you can—the same way you look at several words at a time when you read English.

- Don't stop if you make a mistake! This becomes a habit and you will get lost in the *chart* (written music). Start counting time (1-2-3-4, 2-2-3-4, 3-2-3-4, 4-2-3-4, etc.) the instant you make a mistake so you will know where to come back in.

- Practice reading with a metronome or drum machine.

- If you are making a lot of mistakes—*slow down*. Slowing down is the panacea for all reading problems. Play only as fast as you can play accurately.

- Practice reading every day. It takes patience, so take your time and don't expect dramatic results. It's more like taking baby steps—after a while you see that you have come a long way.

- Use clarinet, violin, flute and sax books to supplement your reading practice.

Put all of the suggestions on page 72 into practice as you work through the next five pages. Enjoy!

(Continued on page 75)

* These are quarter-note triplets. Play three quarter notes in the time of two. Here's a way to count it (play on the underlined counts): **1** trip-**let**, 2 **trip**-let. Just count two eighth-note triplets and play on every other count. Also, it is helpful to start thinking in eighth-note triplets in the last beat of the previous bar.

SECTION IV — BETTER TECHNIQUE

Everybody wants better technique. We all want to be able to translate our ideas into an effortless stream of notes and chords. It is entirely possible for you to develop your skills and talent to your full potential. The first thing though, is that you must be completely honest with yourself about your abilities. Ask yourself these questions:

- What are your main technical weaknesses?
- Does your picking sound nice and even, or is it usually choppy?
- How's your timing? Do your left-hand fingers get to the strings long before your pick is ready to strike? Or vice versa?
- How are your fingerstyle chops?
- How is your chord technique? Do your chord changes have a nice legato flow, or do you struggle from chord to chord? Can you ease into physically difficult chord shapes?

These are the usual problems we see at a jazz skills seminar. Usually, we devote an hour to technique before we get on with the rest of the day's work. I suggest you spend at least some time on technical studies before you begin your other daily practice routines.

On the following pages, you will find quite a few exercises that I have found helpful for most students. They address many of the usual problems that guitarists have. You will find that your technique will improve quickly in some areas and very slowly in others. It is something you must work on and maintain your entire life. Your technique is either "improving" or "getting worse"—it will never remain static. You will find dozens more exercises in my book, *30-Day Guitar Workout*.

Before we get to the actual exercises, we should talk about some other related issues. Some of these may not seem that important by themselves, but together they can make a big difference in your playing.

POSTURE

Better posture means better technique. It doesn't matter if you are playing the guitar or playing baseball. Better form means better performance. Your body is meant to work optimally when your back is straight and you are relaxing any part of your body that doesn't happen to be involved with the task at hand. Be sure not to slouch, lay the guitar flat on your lap or rest your left forearm on your thigh. Sit upright and slightly forward—relax and breathe. Try to practice in the same chair every day. This will make your positioning consistent.

Always wear a guitar strap. The strap holds the guitar for you while your hands do the playing. Your hands function more freely when you wear a strap. Adjust your strap so that the guitar's height relative to your body is exactly the same whether you are standing or sitting.

LEFT HAND

Most of the time, the ball of your thumb should remain along the back of the neck in "hitchhiking" position (pointed away from you). It is natural for the thumb to "go where it wants to go" while playing, but the idea is to try to keep your thumb in back of the neck. This will allow you to arch your wrist out a little, giving your fingers better leverage and keeping all of the strings right under your fingertips. If your thumb were wrapped around the neck, the lower strings would be harder to reach. Your fingers should go straight down to any string. Once you get used to this position, you should notice a greater level of agility.

Try to play with your fingertips instead of the pads. Your finger's job is to press the string against the fret, so make sure your fingertips are placed firmly just behind the fret wire. If your fingers are placed correctly, you will find that much less pressure is required to sound a note. Keep your fingers hovering no more than a quarter inch above the strings. This will help smooth out your playing—especially at faster tempos.

Try to play single notes with a *legato* (smooth, flowing) sound. Each note should be sustained for its fullest value—until the next note is sounded. You can develop this technique by practicing scales or licks very slowly, being careful to leave your finger on a note until just after the next note has been struck. In time, this will become natural and you'll be able to play this way at any tempo. If you think your playing sounds a little choppy, spend some time concentrating on legato technique. That should go a long way in solving the problem.

RIGHT HAND

PICK STYLE

If you are working on the material in this book, you don't really need to be told how to hold a pick. Below are some suggestions on a few related topics.

- Generally, it is not a good idea to use very large picks. The standard, triangular-style or smaller is recommended.

- Learn all styles of picking. Learn to use alternate, circular (see page 82) and sweep picking (if any of these terms is unfamiliar, you should pick up a good technique book). Keep your "up" strokes the same volume and tone as your "down" strokes.

- Keep your entire right arm relaxed. Most of your "picking action" should come from your thumb and forefinger.

FINGERSTYLE

Keep your right arm relaxed from your shoulder all the way down to your fingertips, your wrist slightly out and your thumb and fingers dipping into the strings. Your elbow should rest on the body of the guitar. Keep your thumb in front of your other fingers. Swing your fingers back into the palm a little after every stroke. Most of the finger motion should come from the middle joints.

LEARNING DIFFICULT CHORDS

If you are having difficulty playing a chord, the first thing to check is your thumb. Try moving it around the back of the neck a bit to see where the rest of your hand feels most comfortable. Repositioning the thumb, even a little, can make a huge difference when learning new and difficult chords.

If you are having trouble producing a good sound because of a difficult stretch:

- Finger the chord as best you can by "relaxing into it." Never try to force it. It is usually easier to plant your 3rd and 4th fingers on their notes and then stretch downward with your 1st and 2nd fingers.
- Hold the chord for a slow count of twenty.
- Release slowly.
- Rest and repeat.

Stretching and holding (along with coordination exercises) is the key to training your hands.

Make sure you always check that all of the voices in the chord are sounding by slowly plucking each string of the chord. It is easy to think you are sounding all the tones even when you're not.

CHANGING DIFFICULT CHORDS

When having difficulty switching from one chord to the next, stop and observe what each finger is doing during the switch. Practice moving each finger from the first chord to the second separately. Start with the 1st finger, then move on to the 2nd, then the 3rd and finally the 4th. Be conscious of the actions you are trying to learn. The ideal move consists of all your fingers exiting the previous chord at the same time and landing on the following chord simultaneously. If you cannot quite accomplish that yet, try using one finger as a pivot finger, landing first to get yourself situated and letting the remaining fingers follow shortly after.

Always practice slowly while learning new material. Learning correctly, with good technique, actually takes less time. Learning in a rush will almost always lead to mistakes and bad habits that will only have to be corrected later.

JAZZ
SKILLS

LEFT HAND EXERCISE

This exercise should be played as slowly as possible. Play the F at the 1st fret of the 6th string. Exert maximum pressure with your 1st finger and hold for a slow count of four. Maintaining this pressure, now add your 2nd finger on F♯. With maximum pressure, count to four again. Add your 3rd finger to G, maintaining the firm pressure with your first two fingers. Hold for four more counts. Now, while maintaining all the pressure, play G♯ with your 4th finger and press hard.

Now, maintain the pressure on fingers 2, 3 and 4 while you move your 1st finger from F on the 6th string to B♭ on the 5th string. Once again, exert maximum pressure with your 1st finger. Continue moving each finger over to the 5th string. Maintain pressure and hold for a count of four each time. When all the fingers are pressing firmly on the 5th string, your 1st finger will move to the 4th string, and so on.

When you finish on the 1st string, relax your hand and rest for a moment before starting the whole thing again from the second fret on the 6th string. Eventually, you should be able to perform this exercise starting from each fret on the 6th string. Remember to always exert maximum pressure during this exercise and count very slowly.

Read the grids from left to right.

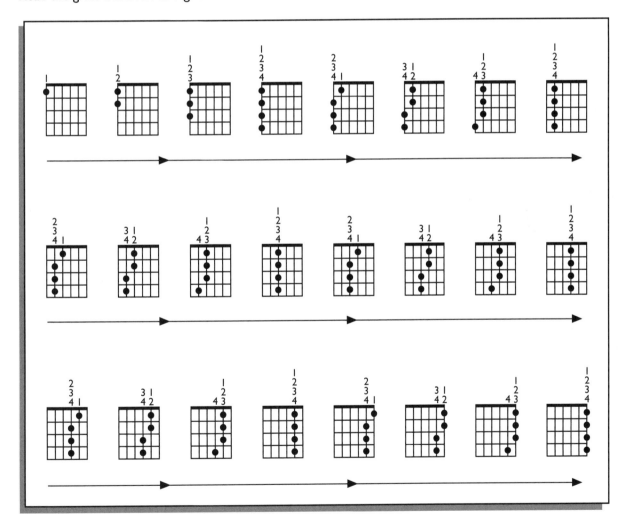

TREMOLO PICKING

On the guitar, *tremolo* is a rapidly repeating note. In this exercise, we slowly (at first) play downstrokes and upstrokes alternately on an open string. The idea is to get both strokes sounding identical in terms of volume and tone. When your notes sound even, speed it up a little. If your picking doesn't sound even, you are going too fast. Working on evenness at progressively faster tempos can attain a good tremolo. Spend two minutes on each string daily.

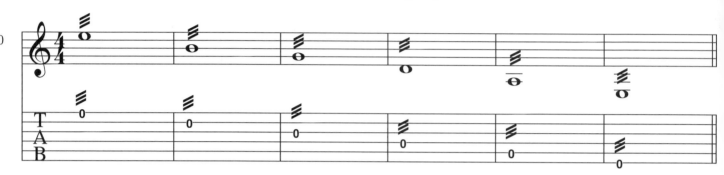

CIRCULAR PICKING

Some guitarists prefer circular picking. It is really the same thing as alternate picking, but you pick in a circular motion. Straighten your thumb and reach forward on the downstroke. Bend your thumb almost 45 degrees and circle back on the upstroke. Hold the pick very loosely. Your thumb and index finger should do all the work. At slower tempos, the circle looks rather large. At faster tempos, the circle is almost imperceptible.

BUILDING STRENGTH

This exercise will build strength in your left hand. Once again, do this exercise very slowly. In fact, the better you get at this exercise, the slower it should go. Play the C at the 8th fret of the 1st string. Hold the note for a slow count of four. Now barre the first two strings (the C on the 1st string and the G on the 2nd string). Hold for four beats, then barre three strings. Hold once again for four beats and then barre four strings. Continue this pattern until you are barring all six strings.

> IMPORTANT: No finger can touch any other finger throughout the duration of this exercise!

Now, work your way back with five strings, four strings, three strings, etc. This is one round. The second round follows the same pattern, only this time you use your 2nd finger. Use your 3rd finger for round three and your 4th finger for round four. Experiment with this exercise on different frets as well.

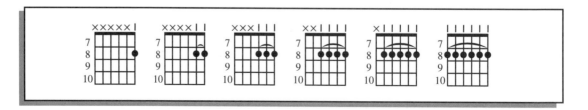

EXERCISES

FINGERSTYLE EXERCISES

Here are the names of the right-hand fingers:

Thumb	=	*p*
Index	=	*i*
Middle	=	*m*
Ring	=	*a*

This is the basic chord shape we'll be working with:

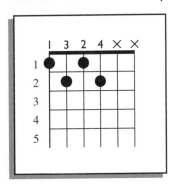

Sound each chord tone in an arpeggio with this fingering: *p-i-m-a-m-i-p*. Move the chord up one fret and repeat the finger pattern. Go all the way up to the highest fret your guitar will accommodate and come back down. Repeat the entire process using this pattern: *p-a-m-i-a-i-p*.

Follow the same procedure on the middle string set with this chord:

Follow the same procedure on the top string set with this chord:

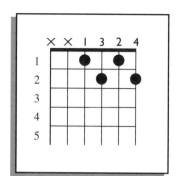

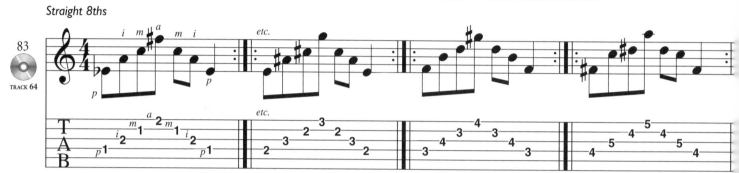

The next step is to apply the *p-i-m-a-m-i-p* pattern to the chord on the low string set twice, then shift to the chord on the middle string set and repeat the pattern twice again. Then move on to the top string set and repeat the pattern twice again. After you finish the pattern on the top string set, move that chord up to the 2nd fret and repeat the picking pattern again. Move to the middle string set, repeat and finally shift over to the bottom string set and repeat the pattern again. Now, move up one fret and continue the pattern across the 3rd fret and on up the entire fingerboard and back down. Strive for an even sound from all right-hand fingers. Play only as quickly as you can while maintaining a clean sound.

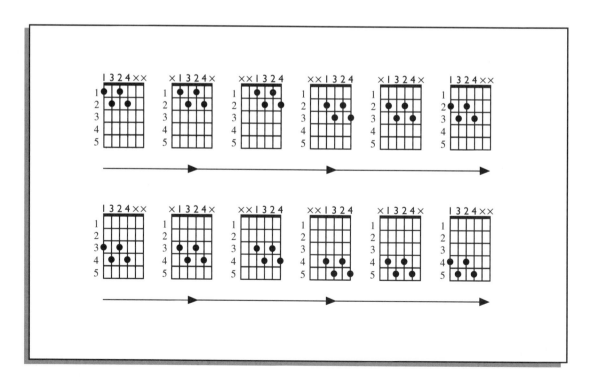

LEFT-HAND DEXTERITY EXERCISE #1

Move this pattern up and down the entire fingerboard chromatically on each string. Start slowly and increase speed. Make sure the open strings are the same volume as the fretted notes. All notes should sound even and the tempo should be steady. Practice the pattern on all six strings.

CHORD EXERCISE #1

The chord exercises in this book are fairly difficult. Memorize them and practice slowly. These can be played with or without a pick.

LEFT-HAND DEXTERITY EXERCISE #2

This is an interesting exercise because when you have played through it once, you have played all twelve major triads in circle of 4ths order. Each 1st finger shift on the 3rd string sets you up for the next move up the fingerboard. Once you have memorized the pattern, start again by placing your 2nd finger on the 2nd fret and moving up the neck from there. Pay attention to the picking!

⊓ = Pick Down

∨ = Pick Up

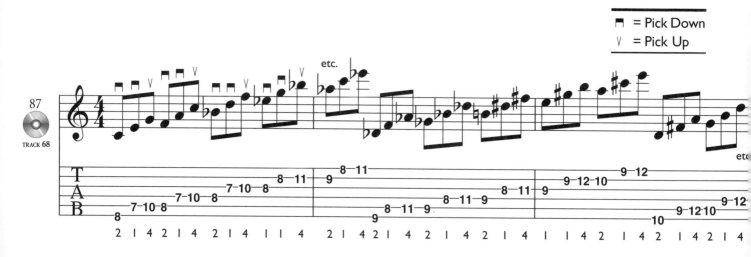

CHORD EXERCISE #2

Many players leave space between their chord changes. They tend to exit a chord early in order to get to the next change in time. The idea here is to get from chord to chord without skimping on any chord's full value. Practice slowly enough to accommodate these moves. Practice ascending and descending in all keys.

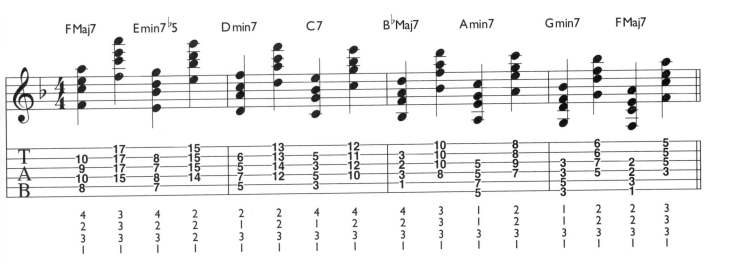

LEFT-HAND DEXTERITY EXERCISE #3

This exercise is a variation of the previous one. Now we are adding the major 7th to each triad by playing the tone that lies one half step below each triad's root. Otherwise, the pattern stays the same. Use alternate picking and pay attention to the fingering.

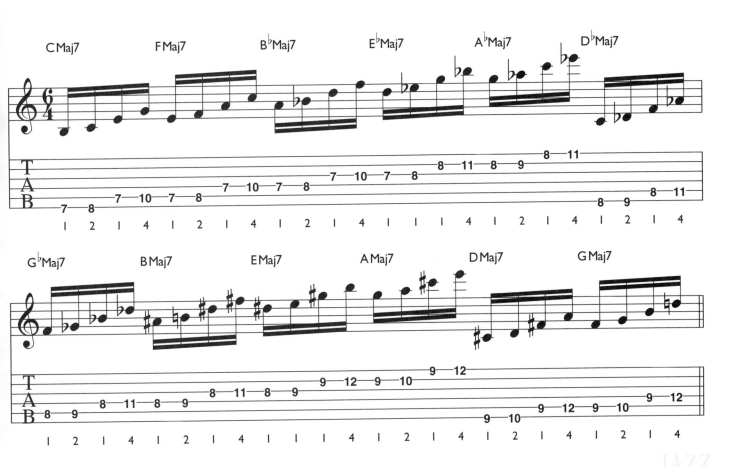

CHORD EXERCISE #3

Below is a chord stretching exercise. Start with this major 7th shape:

Move each finger down one fret, one finger at a time, starting with your 1st finger, then 2nd, etc. The idea is to do this very slowly, so you have to hold the chord down for a while. Try to slide each finger down without lifting off of any note. Start at the top of the fingerboard and travel all the way down to the 1st fret.

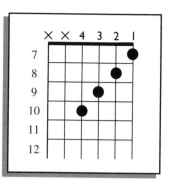

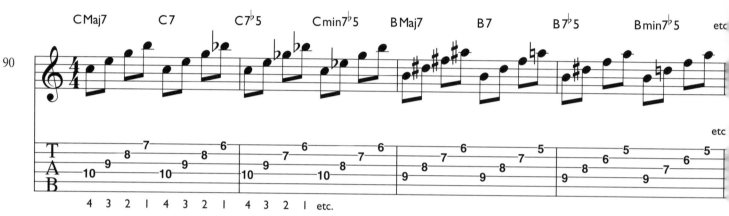

DEXTERITY EXERCISE #4

This is an exercise that will increase the span between the first two fingers of your left hand. Read across the guitar grids from left to right and then continue down the fingerboard. One move needs explanation: when you place your 4th finger down, your 1st finger slides back one fret as all other fingers remain where they are. This is done as one motion. It is as if your 1st finger is shot backward by placing your 4th finger down. This position is held for a slow count of four. Decrease speed as you become more proficient with this. Start on the 9th fret and slowly work your way down.

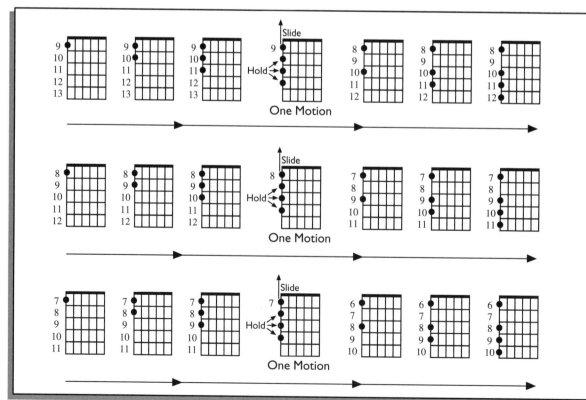

CHORD EXERCISE #4

Here is a four-bar etude. Memorize and practice.

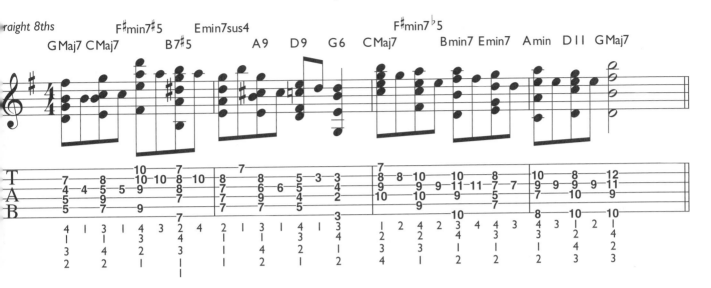

DEXTERITY EXERCISE #5

These are three-note diagonals. The fingerboard can be divided into four string sets of three strings each. First, follow the pattern ascending and descending the fingerboard on individual string sets. Then try crossing the strings sets. In other words, play the pattern ascending at the first fret across all string sets. Then move up to the 2nd fret and play the pattern descending across the string sets in the opposite direction. Weave your way up and down the entire fingerboard. Go slowly at first.

CHORD EXERCISE #5

This exercise combines block chords with arpeggios. Observe the fingerings and play with clarity. Try to maintain a steady tempo. Switching from chords to notes (and vice versa) can be tricky. Practice carefully. Chords and notes should be played at exactly the same volume.

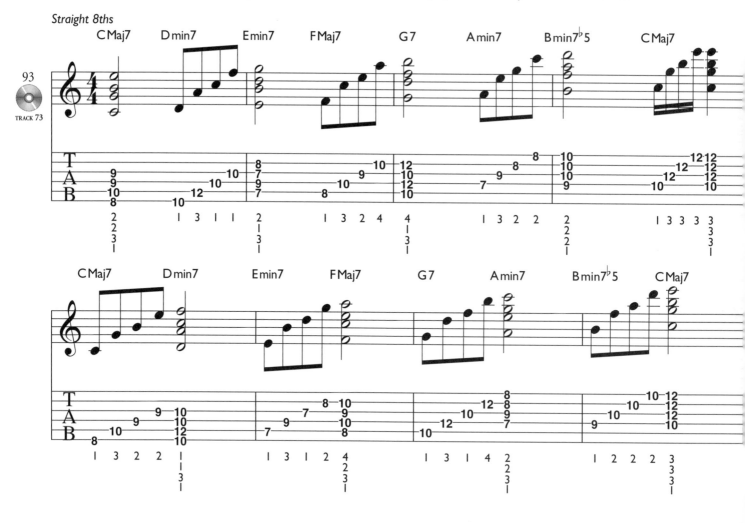

DEXTERITY EXERCISE #6

The exercise at the top of page 91 will help you with a technique called *the roll*. When you have to move from one note to another on the same fret of an adjacent string, it is much more efficient to roll into that second note than to lift your finger off the first note and then place it on the next. To achieve an ascending roll, the first note is played with your fingertip. The second note is fingered by collapsing the top knuckle of the same finger so that the pad is covering the note on the adjacent string. Do not let the first note sustain through the second—just release a little pressure from the first note. A descending roll is accomplished by playing the higher note with the pad of your finger and "standing" that finger up (snapping the top joint into place) so that the second note is being played with the fingertip.

CHORD EXERCISE #6

The following exercise is constructed from the intervals of tritones (♭5) and 4ths. By moving the tritone down by half steps, you are actually playing dominant chords around the circle of 4ths. Practice this from the highest fret your fingerboard will accommodate and travel down and then back up.

AFTERWORDS

PROPER ATTITUDE

Being exposed to so much information during a week-long seminar, or seeing it all together in one short book, can leave one feeling a little overwhelmed. Learning anything new is always a two-step process. First, you need to learn new material intellectually and develop skills. Secondly, you need to merge this new information with the other skills and knowledge you already have. A lot of players already feel like there is too much to learn and practice—how can they add more to the list? A little perspective is in order.

Whether you are a professional or a serious student, you will probably study and play the guitar for many, many years. You will probably find that you are attracted to different styles and techniques at different times of your life. A lot of schools and teachers advocate a rigorous practice schedule in which one would practice *everything* every day! This would include chords, theory, improvisation, technique reading, ear training, learning tunes (maybe composing) and active listening. This is probably unrealistic for most people.

I will make specific practice suggestions in this section about practicing. You need to try and strike a balance between all the things there are to accomplish in music with what is actually possible, given your own unique situation. You have to realize that jazz guitar is a lifetime study. It is better to work in one or two areas that really interest you than to try to study everything you *think* you should. If you're a professional, you need to practice for your gig. Regardless of category, work only on one or two things at a time until they sound great—then move on to something else. You'll know what to work on if you listen to your intuition. If you really don't know, have a good teacher suggest a few things to work on. Progress doesn't usually happen in giant leaps. It's more like baby steps—after a while, you realize you've actually come a long way. Enjoy the journey, since there is no final destination.

INITIALIZING CONCEPTS

Books are fine. Videos are cool. Both can be great sources of information. Neither will make you a great player. What makes a great player is experience in playing and listening. If you want to play well, you absolutely have to get out there and play with others.

Some students are literally glued to their books. They study and turn pages and wonder why they don't improve. You have to learn the lesson from the book (or video or teacher) and then *get away from the book*. You need to start applying all new information right away. Let's say you need some new voicings for minor ii-V7-i progressions. You open your book and learn a few. Now—close the book and work these new voicings into songs that you already know. Or, learn a new tune and use the new voicings as part of your arrangement. Lessons and instructional material won't do you any good unless you memorize and apply.

Your new mantra: ***Memorize and Apply!***

WHAT TO LEARN AND IN WHAT ORDER

Years ago, there were no guitar schools. Jazz guitar books were rare. Good jazz guitar books were *really* rare. Somebody would show you something and you would go home and work on it, internalize it and then look for more information. In some ways this was good because you weren't flooded with information. You had time to develop your ideas before you ran across any new information. The downside, of course, is that whatever you picked up was not usually in any particular order. Sometimes it would take a few years before you could see how it all fit together.

Generally, you should work on things in the order shown below. Your unique needs will dictate where to start on this list:

Major Scales
Triads
Larger Chord Formulas
Harmonized Major Scales
Comping
Improvising with Major Scales
ii-V7-I Progressions
Diatonic Arpeggios
Neighbor Tones
Licks
Modes of the Major Scale
Altered Chords
Improvising over Altered Chords
Modes of the Melodic Minor Scale
Modes of the Harmonic Minor Scale
Chord/Melody

No list like this can be complete or accurate for everyone. In addition to the listed topics, you also need to spend time transcribing and learning tunes, not to mention working on your ear and technique. This list makes sense because the knowledge you gain in one topic will help you understand the next one. There is no *one* true way—shop around and find out what works best for you.

PRACTICE

There are really two kinds of practice: conceptual and motor skills. You are practicing conceptually when you are learning new material: a song, a scale or lick, a chord voicing—or anything else for that matter. If you put all your effort into it, 20 minutes of continuous concentration is a long time and a lot can be learned. One or two of these sessions daily and you could learn an awful lot in one year. Try not to be interrupted. Stay focused. Memorize *while* you learn. The sooner you get away from the written music, the sooner you make the new material *your own*.

When you are perfecting or maintaining songs, arpeggios, licks, chords or anything else, you are practicing your motor skills. Most great players will tell you that there have been periods of their lives that included hours and hours of practice every day.

When you are practicing things like scales, try to have fun. Don't just play straight eighth notes. Play them in $\frac{4}{4}, \frac{3}{4}, \frac{6}{8}, \frac{7}{8}$. Play them with different feels: sambas, swing, ballads. Get creative with new materials right away.

Sometimes, taking a day off from practice can be good for your playing. You gain a fresher view of the things you are working on.

Practice in all keys.

Practice slowly.

TUNING

A lot of guitar players are a little self-conscious about tuning. For some reason, they think they need to tune really fast, especially if there is another guitar player watching. You should take your time tuning Everything you do after that depends on it.

Using a tuner is a good idea when you are trying to tune in a noisy room or during a recording session. Don't be "tuner dependent," though. You should be able to tune by ear. Realize that your ear changes a little from day to day. Don't be afraid to tune slowly and accurately.

LEARNING TUNES

For some reason, a lot of guitar players never really learn a lot of tunes. The most important things to practice are your songs. You should always be updating your repertoire. The whole point of all the theory, fingerboard studies and exercises is to *play songs*.

WHICH SONGS?

There are many good jazz *fake books* out there. (Some of them are illegal—they are clear violations of the songwriters' rights.) Learn the songs you hear your favorite players play. Learn the tunes you didn't know last night when the bandleader called them or when someone requested them. Unless you are writing your own tunes, most songs will fall into the following categories:

> Straight ahead (swing)
> Latin
> Straight eighth-note feels
> Ballads

You know the tune fully when:

- You have memorized the melody in single notes, in every octave.

- You have memorized and can play all the chord changes in at least three areas on the fingerboard.

- You can play the chord changes in any key.

- You have spent time improvising over the changes. The problem spots have been ironed out, and you can navigate the changes competently.

- You can play it at any tempo.

Work up chord/melody arrangements for the tunes you really like a lot.

Keep working, learning and playing. Enjoy!

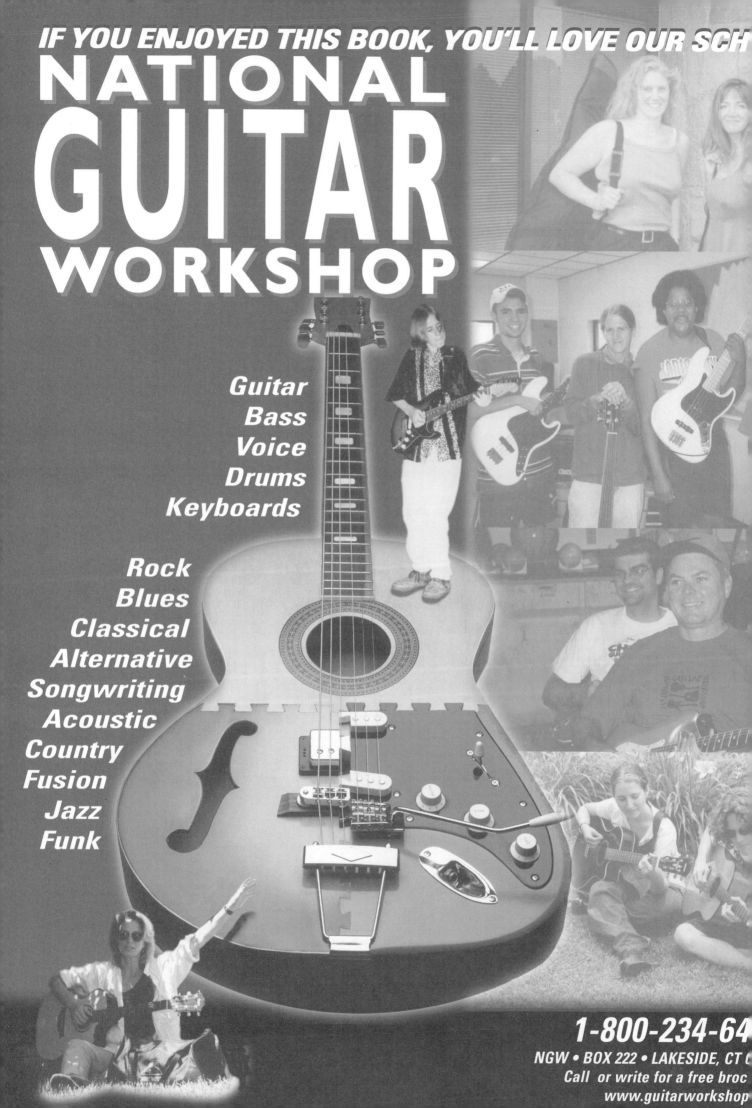